Back To The Facts
Part 1

James Mitchell

INTRODUCTION

At least since Donald Trump became president of the United States the term "Fake News" has become a synonym for everything that's wrong in our society. People cannot trust each other anymore and people specifically do not trust newspapers anymore. In a world where people start to trust strangers in shaky YouTube videos more than ever, we thought we must stop this development. We therefore roamed the continents and dug deep into many different subject areas on our search to uncover the real truth. The outcome is this book which tells you the facts that matter and that are far away from being fake news.

We hope this will give you a plenty of joy and more than a few surprises. Enjoy the read!

BACK TO THE FACTS – PART 1

Fact 1: Actor Robert Downey Jr. credits Burger King with saving his life. When he wanted to eat a burger from the fast food chain in 2003, he found it so bad that he began rethinking his entire life and decided to put an end to his drug addiction. Five years later, he received the role of Iron Man.

Fact 2: If you write "3:)" on Facebook you will see a little surprise.

Fact 3: All time zones meet in Antarctica, so it is almost impossible to attribute an exact time to the place. Instead, the time of the country owning the respective research station is often used for simplification purposes.

Fact 4: From a water depth of 33 feet and more it becomes impossible to fart.

Fact 5: A few hours after an infection with HIV, post-exposure prophylaxis which can significantly reduce the risk of contracting the virus is possible.

Fact 6: Scientists at the Massachusetts Institute of Technology have developed a tattoo ink that changes color when a person is dehydrated or when his or her blood sugar level is too high.

Fact 7: In North Korea, basketball is played according to different rules. For example, the team loses points if it doesn't score on free throws and a dunk scores three points instead of the usual two.

Fact 8: Skateboard professional Tony Hawk has an IQ of 144.

Fact 9: Joy Milne from Britain has the ability to recognize whether somebody is suffering from Parkinson's by smell. In a scientific test, she identified the six people among the twelve test subjects who suffered from Parkinson's disease based only on their smell. However, she also claimed that a seventh person who was actually part of the control group had the disease. Later on, this person was also diagnosed with Parkinson's, so that Joy ultimately passed the test without a single error. To this day, scientists do not know how Joy Milne's ability works, but they hope to use this knowledge to find new ways to detect Parkinson's disease.

Fact 10: The average income of an intern at Facebook and Snapchat is between 8,000 to 10,000 dollars a month.

Fact 11: "Jenga" is Swahili and means "to build".

Fact 12: Humans are the only species that cook their food.

Fact 13: The risk of drowning in the desert is greater than the risk of dying of thirst there. Occasionally, there can be heavy rain in deserts, and as the water cannot seep away due to the dryness of the soil, it produces deadly flash floods.

Fact 14: Sunsets on Mars appear in a blue tone.

Fact 15: Apple was the first private company to reach a market value of a trillion dollars.

Fact 16: A human could survive two minutes in space without a space suit.

Fact 17: In Russia, there are approximately eleven million more women than men.

Fact 18: The Australian state of Queensland allows emojis on license plates.

Fact 19: A nap of six minutes at midday improves memory capacity significantly.

Fact 20: Hippopotami on average kill 2,900 humans per year, stags 130, ants 30, cows 22, horses 20 and sharks only five. But who would run away from a cow?

Fact 21: In terms of stress levels people aged 18-33 face the hardest challenges.

Fact 22: For every episode of "The Simpsons" the producers needed six to nine months.

Fact 23: In Germany, almost each second marriage ends in divorce.

Fact 24: Cats sweat through their paws.

Fact 25: In the 19th and 20th centuries, a family clan with predominantly bluish skin lived in the Appalachian Mountains in the USA. This was due to a disease called methemoglobinemia, which was repeatedly passed on within the Fugate family due to the isolated living conditions in the mountains.

Fact 26: An anonymous donor pays for the college tuition of each student in Kalamazoo, Michigan.

Fact 27: A bite of the Brazilian wandering spider can cause men an erection that lasts for hours.

Fact 28: In the middle of Lake Taal on the island of Luzan, which belongs to the Philippines, lies Volcano Island, which is home to a crater lake which in turn contains a small island called Volcano Point. It is therefore an island in a lake on an island in a lake on an island.

Fact 29: For his role as Iron Man, Robert Downey Jr. was paid 500,000 dollars in the first part. For the first Avengers film, however, his pay had already increased to 50 million dollars.

Fact 30: A behavioral study came to the conclusion that brunette women are perceived as more intelligent by their peers than women with other hair colors.

Fact 31: During the filming of "Wonder Woman", actress Gal Gadot was already five months pregnant. In order to conceal her baby belly, her armor was replaced by green fabric during the shoot and later digitally replaced by a non-pregnant belly.

Fact 32: Female skunks are able to influence the development of their embryos, in order to delay birth in times of food shortages.

Fact 33: In the U.S., the probability of suicide is twice the rate of an assassination by a third party.

Fact 34: All Scandinavian countries have a cross on their flag.

Fact 35: The Lily actress Alyson Hannigan from "How I Met Your Mother" is married to Alexis Dennis in real life, the actor of news reader Sandy Rivers.

Fact 36: An iPad with apps installed weighs more than an iPad without apps installed.

Fact 37: In 1967, a former Prime Minister of Australia disappeared without a trace and has still not been found.

Fact 38: McDonald's also delivers its food - in at least 18 countries around the world.

Fact 39: Babies are born with 300 bones. In adulthood this number decreases to 206.

Fact 40: About 80 percent of people breathe exclusively through one nostril. Which nostril is used by the body varies approximately every 2.5 hours. While the other nostril is not being used for breathing, the body cleans it.

Fact 41: A long, thin string is stretched around a part of Manhattan, used by the Jewish population for orientation on the Sabbath.

Fact 42: The longest prison sentence a man ever received was 384,912 years. The sentence was received by a 22 year old postman, who had not delivered over 42,000 letters.

Fact 43: People who laugh more frequently, live a longer life.

Fact 44: When explorers Lewis and Clark undertook the first American overland expedition from the United States to the Pacific coast, they needed a number of translators to communicate with the Indian tribes. The translators translated from English to French, to Hidatsa, to Shoshoni and finally to Salish.

Fact 45: The inventor of the Game Boy was initially a janitor at Nintendo.

Fact 46: In Australia in 2009, snipers were tasked with defending a colony of penguins against possible enemies to guarantee the survival of this rare penguin species.

Fact 47: In Minneapolis, Minnesota, a room has been developed, for research purposes, that absorbs all sounds. If you are inside, it is so quiet that you can even hear your own pulse. However, if you stay too long in absolute silence, hallucinations may occur.

Fact 48: The book "Everything men know about woman" consists of 100 blank pages.

Fact 49: Professional US swimmer Michael Phelps has won more gold medals than 80 percent of all countries in the history of the Olympic Games.

Fact 50: The actor Morgan Freeman has already been nominated for more prizes than he has made films.

Fact 51: In the 17th century, New York was called New Amsterdam.

Fact 52: In 1975, the American Gary Dahl sold so-called "Pet Rocks". These were just common pebbles, but Dahl marketed them like pets. Within a very short time, a big hype arose about the stones, quickly making Dahl a millionaire. Only one year later, however, the interest quickly subsided again.

Fact 53: The Swedish man Max Martin is the most successful music composer in the world. Among others he wrote the songs "Wish You Were Here", "Quit Playing Games With My Heart", "I Want You Back", "Oops! ... I Did It Again", "It's My Life", "Since U Been Gone", "I Kissed a Girl", "Hot n Cold", "Dynamite", "DJ Got Us Falling' in Love" and "Fucking Perfect".

Fact 54: Slugs are able to sleep three consecutive years.

Fact 55: The word "Swagger" is a neologism and was created by William Shakespeare.

Fact 56: The "L" in Samuel L. Jackson's name stands for "Leroy".

Fact 57: Besides humans, ants and bees are the only animals to wage war against members of the same species.

Fact 58: Only 14 percent of all billionaires have no degree.

Fact 59: African American Ebbie Tolbert was born in 1807 and lived in slavery for more than 50 years. At the advanced age of 113 years - shortly before her death - she was allowed to cast her ballot for the first time in her life in St. Louis.

Fact 60: The first Game Boy had as much computing power needed as for the first moon landing.

Fact 61: More than 50% if the world's French speaking population lives in Africa.

Fact 62: Google employees are allowed to use 20 percent of their working time every day for their own individual side projects. Among other things, this has led to the development of Google News.

Fact 63: 32-year-old Wombat "Patrick" living in Australia was the oldest animal of his species. As he was not able to find a female partner, his keepers even created a Tinder profile for him.

Fact 64: Foxes use the Earth's magnetic field to estimate distances.

Fact 65: It took one year to sell a million copies of the first iPhone. With the iPhone 6, a million copies were sold on the first weekend of its release.

Fact 66: After Josef Stalin had heard that his son failed to commit suicide, he said: "He can't even shoot straight."

Fact 67: Multimillionaire Forrest Fenn, hid a treasure worth two million dollars in the Rocky Mountains. In order to find it, you have to solve a number of puzzles. Until today, nobody has found the treasure.

Fact 68: In the first season of the Simpsons, Bart's school was still purple, Moe and Chief Wiggum's hair was black, and donuts were called "Kringel" in the German version.

Fact 69: When Erich Honecker, a GDR politician, first visited the Federal Republic of Germany, his red carpet was 8 inches shorter than usual, because the Federal Republic did not want to show him the same respect as other citizens and friends.

Fact 70: Scorpions can survive for up to one year without food.

Fact 71: Based on crime statistics, Tokyo is the safest city in the world.

Fact 72: When the USA bought Alaska from Russia in 1867, they switched from the Julian calendar previously used in Alaska to the Gregorian calendar used in the USA. The result was that the 8th to 17th of October 1867 never existed in Alaska.

Fact 73: In Germany, there is a woman named "Pepsi-Carola". Shortly after her birth on 4 May 1959, while still at the hospital, she was sponsored by PepsiCo. Under this special promotional campaign, she received an educational endowment insurance of 6,000 Deutschmarks, while her parents received a cash sum of 4,000 Deutschmarks.

Fact 74: About 90 percent of all lung cancer cases are caused by smoking.

Fact 75: In 2013, more people died in the United States from children playing with small guns than from terrorists

Fact 76: NBA athlete Allen Iverson signed a lifetime advertising contract with Reebok in 2001. For this he will receive an annual sum of 800,000 dollars until he is 55 years old. After that, he will receive a single lump sum of 32 million dollars from the company.

Fact 77: In the special edition 3 of the Club Nintendo comic book series, the reader finds out that Kirby smokes, drinks and eats unhealthy fast food.

Fact 78: A Stanford University study found that marijuana users on average have sex about 20 percent more often than people who do not consume marijuana.

Fact 79: Goosebumps are a reflex from the times when man had much more hair. When our hair stands up, we appeared bigger and more menacing to enemies.

Fact 80: "Samhainophobia" is the fear of Halloween.

Fact 81: The equal sign "=" was invented in 1557 by Robert Recorde.

Fact 82: A Jamais-vu is the opposite of a Déjà-vu.

Fact 83: In 2018, bitcoin mining already consumed as much electricity as the entire Czech Republic.

Fact 84: Dubai uses falcons to keep their cities free of pigeons.

Fact 85: Bulls cannot see the color red at all.

Fact 86: Nowadays, 82 percent of young people do not ring doors anymore, but send a message that they have arrived and wait outside the door.

Fact 87: In space you cannot burp.

Fact 88: During the First World War, a unique event took place on the western front. On Christmas Eve, allied troops stopped their fighting and started singing Christmas carols. The Germans responded by shouting "Merry Christmas". Some of the English then came out of their trenches and ran to the Germans to greet them and shake hands, and then the soldiers even exchanged cigarettes.

Fact 89: Walter Arnold was the first person to pay a fine for speeding. In 1896, he drove his car through a zone with speed restrictions at 7.5 miles per hour, clearly exceeding the speed limit of 1.7 miles per hour.

Fact 90: When in 1940 Adolf Hitler banned the public display of colored people in Germany, he was the first state leader to take action against the so-called "human zoos".

Fact 91: The word "Arctic" comes from Greek and means "bear", while "Antarctic" stands for "opposite the Arctic". By this, the Greeks wanted to express that the star constellations of the Big Dipper and the Little Dipper, call Big Bear and Small Bear in Greek, are visible in the northern hemisphere, but cannot be seen in the southern hemisphere.

Fact 92: Mangalica pigs are a rare type of pig that due to their curly, light bristles look like sheep.

Fact 93: Humans do not develop exclusively through the genetic mixture of mother and father. On average, every human is born with about 100 mutations.

Fact 94: In Ukraine there is a 1,000 feet deep salt mine, which is used in the treatment of respiratory diseases. Due to the high salt content, there are fewer bacteria in the air than compared to the most sterile rooms of a hospital.

Fact 95: Brooklyn "Brookie" Supreme is considered the largest horse to ever have existed. It was almost 6.6 feet tall and weighed over 1.5 tons.

Fact 96: Mental tasks that require a particularly intensive involvement of short-term memory, usually lead to an interruption of all bodily activity. For example, if you are taking a walk with a friend and ask them to multiply 73 by 28, they will, in most cases, stop suddenly to solve the problem.

Fact 97: The birth rate in Japan is so low that the number of adult diapers sold now exceeds the number of baby diapers sold.

Fact 98: On January 1 1985, the first phone call was made using a cellular phone.

Fact 99: In the USA, a slave from 1850 by today's standards, would cost 1,000 dollars.

Fact 100: Arnold Schwarzenegger was meant to play the role of Kyle Reese in the movie "Terminator".

Fact 101: In 1985, a school child named Ryan White was not allowed to attend class because he had AIDS. About 117 parents and 50 teachers signed a petition for this. Some parents even ended their newspaper subscription, as Ryan White was their paper boy and they believed they could get infected.

Fact 102: In Newfoundland (Canada) there is a city called Dildo.

Fact 103: The American author Mark Twain's real name was Samuel Langhorne Clemens.

Fact 104: In Novosibirsk, Russia, there is a monument to all laboratory mice in the world. The statue shows a mouse wearing a lab coat knitting a DNA helix to commemorate all laboratory mice and rats that died in the name of science.

Fact 105: After the first drive-in was opened at McDonald's in China, the system was so strange to the Chinese people that many people ordered their food from their car, parked their vehicle and then went to the restaurant to eat.

Fact 106: The world record for the most push-ups in one day is 46,001.

Fact 107: Netflix now accounts for about 15 percent of all Internet traffic in the United States.

Fact 108: Pandas are able to fake a pregnancy to get more food from the zookeepers.

Fact 109: The most frequently visited tourist attraction in Paris is not the Eiffel Tower or the Louvre, but Disneyland.

Fact 110: The Titanoboa was the largest snake to ever have lived. The 46-foot-long animal, which weighed more than 1.3 tons, haunted the Colombian rainforest some 60 million years ago.

Fact 111: If one donates a part of one's liver, the missing part will grow again.

Fact 112: On average, there are 88.8 weapons per 100 U.S. citizens.

Fact 113: If you could power an iPhone with gasoline, one drop would be enough to use the smartphone for a whole day.

Fact 114: The phenomenon that people forget things which are easy to look up on Google, is called the "Google Effect".

Fact 115: Django Unchained was the first movie in sixteen years in which Leonardo DiCaprio wasn't the highest paid actor on set.

Fact 116: In 1879 the Belgian mail service launched a pilot project in which cats were used to deliver the letters. The project failed.

Fact 117: Edgar Bergen was the first man to win an Oscar made of wood for his ventriloquial performance.

Fact 118: In 1973, the American David Rosenhan had eleven mentally healthy people admitted to psychiatric institutions in an experiment, without informing the treating physicians that the patients were healthy. The test subjects were held in the institutions for up to 52 days. One was diagnosed with schizophrenia and another with manic-depressive psychosis.

Fact 119: In chess, there is a way to checkmate your opponent in two moves. If a player wins with this strategy, it is called a "Fool's Mate".

Fact 120: In the early 50s a "Blow Job" described the bang when breaking the sound barrier.

Fact 121: Since no human has ever seen or heard a live dinosaur, all the sounds of dinosaurs known from movies are completely imaginary. There is no evidence that dinosaurs really sounded that way.

Fact 122: The actor Mark Wahlberg was suspended from school after just a few years and therefore never finished it. To be a shining example to his kids, he catched up on his high school diploma in the age of 42.

Fact 123: Short female car drivers have the highest likelihood of being killed by the cars airbag due to their close distance to the steering wheel.

Fact 124: Rice has more genes than humans.

Fact 125: Nothing is an uninhabited town in the U.S. state of Arizona. There is nothing but a gas station and a garage.

Fact 126: During the Second World War, the city of Constance was largely spared from Allied bombing raids. Unlike other German cities, Constance did not cut off electricity at night. Allied pilots could therefore hardly distinguish the city from neighboring Switzerland, where the lights also remained on at night. In order to avoid mistakes, no bombs were dropped in the region.

Fact 127: The "Gombe Chimpanzee War" describes a four-year war between two hostile chimpanzee groups in Tanzania. During this time, there were mutual killings, violence and kidnappings. The war is considered the first known situation in which chimpanzees deliberately killed another chimpanzee.

Fact 128: Elephants are able to recognize themselves in a mirror. Even most primates do not have this mental capacity.

Fact 129: Irv Gordon holds the record for the longest distance a person has ever driven in the same car. He bought a Volvo P1800 in 1966 and has driven more than 3,2 million miles since then.

Fact 130: Jessica Cox was born without arms and in 2008 became the first person with this disability to be officially licensed as a pilot. In addition to this, she is also a Taekwondo black belt.

Fact 131: "Pikachurin" is a protein that facilitates the correct transmission of electrical signals between the eye and the brain. It was discovered by Japanese scientists and named after the Pokémon Pikachu.

Fact 132: Venus rotates around its own axis at only four miles per hour. So you could walk around Venus faster than it can turn itself.

Fact 133: A piece of biscuit that survived the sinking of the Titanic was auctioned for over 15,000 pounds. The biscuit was 103 years old at the time.

Fact 134: According to the Global Age Watch Index 2014, Germany is the third best country on earth after Sweden and Norway, for humans to get as old as possible.

Fact 135: Students get better test results when looking at a green landscape during the test.

Fact 136: The sun is actually white. But our atmosphere makes it look yellowish to us.

Fact 137: The largest dog in the world is 43.7 inches tall.

Fact 138: Vagina is the Latin word for "shcath".

Fact 139: Everything you write into your Facebook status, is irreversibly sent to Facebook - regardless if you actually post it.

Fact 140: Nazi Germany was the first country in the world to launch an anti-smoking campaign. Soldiers, for example, were forbidden to smoke while on duty.

Fact 141: Financially, World War I did not end for Germany until 2010, when the last of the reparations payments under the Treaty of Versailles was made.

Fact 142: The largest volcano in the world - the Tamu Massif in the Pacific - has an area roughly the size of Great Britain and Ireland combined.

Fact 143: Due to strong solar storms in 1859, the earth experienced the strongest geomagnetic storm ever recorded. The storm was so strong that you could see auroras even in Rome and some telegraphs could be operated for more than two hours without being connected to the power grid, using only the energy produced by the geomagnetic storm.

Fact 144: The so-called urchin crab (Dorippe frascone) carries sea urchins on its back to defend itself.

Fact 145: A pineapple was such a large status symbol in 18th century England that you could rent it for a day.

Fact 146: In Lazio (Italy) policemen drive Lamborghinis.

Fact 147: In 90 percent of all adoption cases in Japan, adoption occurs among people who are already of age. The main reason is that older businessmen in particular need a successor for their family business.

Fact 148: Excessive sleep deprivation can lead to obesity.

Fact 149: Zebras and ostriches often stay together in the wilderness. Ostriches can see enemies at long distances, while zebras are able to hear enemies from far away.

Fact 150: In 1980 a hospital in Las Vegas had to dismiss several employees as they were betting on when patients would die.

Fact 151: In ancient Egypt, meteorite rocks were used as jewels.

Fact 152: According to a social study conducted by Arizona State University, men think they are smarter than equally smart women. Women, on the other hand, tend to underestimate their abilities.

Fact 153: With a height of 59 feet, the tallest animal to ever have lived on earth was probably the Sauroposeidon. One of its cervical vertebrae alone was already 4.6 feet long.

Fact 154: Mexican priest Sergio Gutiérrez Benítez supported an orphanage for over 23 years by earning money as a wrestler under the pseudonym "Fray Tormenta". He became known all over the world for his distinctive mask, which he now wears even during his sermons in church.

Fact 155: When the height of Mount Everest was first determined in the 19th century, researchers calculated a total height of exactly 29,000 feet. The height they published, however, was 29,002 feet, as the researchers feared that a figure as even as 29,000 feet might be interpreted as a rough estimate.

Fact 156: Gnats are especially attracted by people with blood type O.

Fact 157: In 2007, a Greenland whale was killed during a whaling expedition. In the animal's body, the tip of a harpoon was found which must have been there since 1885. This discovery proved that the animal must have been more than 130 years old and confirmed the hypothesis that the Greenland whale is the mammal with the highest life expectancy.

Fact 158: More than 800 castles are currently on sale in France.

Fact 159: The vaginal fluid of women can be found in sharks.

Fact 160: If McDonald's was its own country, it would be the 90th biggest economy in the world.

Fact 161: The average price of one liter of black ink is higher than the price of one liter of human blood.

Fact 162: The 100 richest people in the world earned so much money last year that they could end global poverty four times over.

Fact 163: The West Indies lie in the Atlantic Ocean, east of Central America.

Fact 164: The urine of the Asian bearcat smells like popcorn. The reason for this is that the animal's urine contains the same fragrance that gives popcorn its distinctive smell.

Fact 165: In 1960, Frances Kelsey, an executive at the U.S. Food and Drug Administration (FDA), refused to approve thalidomide as a painkiller for pregnant women, even though the drug had already been approved in more than 20 other Western countries. Later on, it was discovered that the drug, marketed under the name "Contergan", caused severe disabilities in children. So Frances Kelsey's decision saved countless children in the United States.

Fact 166: Cats cannot taste sugar.

Fact 167: It is not possible to eat 30 salt sticks within one minute.

Fact 168: At the beginning of the 20th century, radium was often used as an ingredient in facial cream.

Fact 169: When Komodo dragons bite their prey, they release a poison that, among other things, inhibits blood clotting. So if their prey is not killed immediately, the dragons can then track it down and feed on it after it has died from blood loss as well as from the other bacteria contained in the poison.

Fact 170: "Cunningham's Law" describes the phenomenon that the fastest way to find a correct answer on the Internet is not to ask the question, but to post the wrong answer.

Fact 171: Although 70 percent of our planet's surface is covered with water, a sphere containing all the water in the world would only have a diameter of about 435 miles. That is less than half the diameter of the moon.

Fact 172: Although Rwanda is listed as #46 least developed country in the world it has a better gender equality than the USA.

Fact 173: Saddam Hussein had a Koran, written with his own blood.

Fact 174: Dolphins sleep with there eyes open.

Fact 175: During the first days in space, astronauts often suffer from space sickness. Since all bodily fluids are redistributed in weightlessness and the sense of balance is impaired, important tasks such as outboard work are not carried out in the first days of a space mission. There would be an acute risk of the astronauts throwing up in their suits.

Fact 176: The number of all possible Sudoku puzzles with a 9x9 field is 6,670,903,752,021,072,936,960, which is about 6.7 sextillion.

Fact 177: With 30 inhabitants, Hum in Croatia is the smallest city in the world.

Fact 178: Your hearing is worse when you are well fed.

Fact 179: Sharks have been living on our planet for more than 420 million years. They existed before the dinosaurs.

Fact 180: The table tennis ball in "Forrest Gump" was inserted by special effect designers, so that Tom Hanks never had to play table tennis.

Fact 181: "Snakes Venom" is the strongest beer in the world with an alcohol content of 67.5 percent. It contains more alcohol than whiskey.

Fact 182: In Las Vegas, Paris and Munich, there are escape games based on the horror movie "SAW".

Fact 183: Sharks and rays are the only animals that cannot develop cancer.

Fact 184: The silk of the spider species "Caeristris darwini" is the toughest biomaterial in the world - ten times stronger than a comparable strand of Kevlar.

Fact 185: In 1724 Maggie Dickson from Scotland was sentenced to death by hanging. After she had been hanged and taken away in a coffin, it turned out that she had survived. A court ruled that the sentence was officially carried out, so she could not be punished any further. She continued to live for over 40 years and was nicknamed "Half-Hangit Maggie".

Fact 186: In 2009 in Florida, a man who was accused of owning child porn, said his cat had downloaded the files.

Fact 187: The longest monosyllabic word in the English language is strengths.

Fact 188: Dubai has an indoor ski center.

Fact 189: In Kenya, elephant droppings are used to make paper. 110 pounds of excrement can be used to produce 125 pages of paper. The proceeds from the sale of the paper are used to expand the elephant reserve.

Fact 190: Our blood accounts for seven percent of our body weight.

Fact 191: If the sum of all the digits of a number is divisible by three, then the number itself can also be divided by three.

Fact 192: With every ejaculation a man unloads one to two teaspoons full of sperm.

Fact 193: Coober Pedy is a city in the Australian outback, where more than 50 percent of the inhabitants live in underground caves.

Fact 194: 300 is the film with the most deaths per minute in film history. On average, more than five people die in one minute.

Fact 195: In the 1990s, the Coca-Cola Company tested vending machines that automatically changed prices depending on the outside temperature. When it was particularly hot, customers had to pay more.

Fact 196: On 24 February 1891, the "United States of Brazil" were founded, and the name of the country lasted for almost 40 years. So at the time, the American continent was home to not only the USA, but also the USB.

Fact 197: Frank Oz, the voice of Yoda in Star Wars, was also the voice of Miss Piggy.

Fact 198: There is a programming language called ArnoldC, which consists only of quotes by Arnold Schwarzenegger.

Fact 199: The Nobel Prizes were established by the Swedish inventor Alfred Nobel. He invented dynamite and went on to become very wealthy because of it. Before dying, he drew up a will stipulating that after his death the majority of his assets were to go to his foundation. The interest generated from these assets is used to award annual Nobel Prizes in physics, chemistry, medicine, literature and peace efforts. They were first awarded in 1901.

Fact 200: The Amazon is home to pink dolphins.

Fact 201: Super Mario was originally a carpenter before he was portrayed as a plumber in later parts of the series.

Fact 202: On 14 May 1939, Lina Medina gave birth to her first child at the age of five years and seven months. To this day, she is considered the youngest mother ever. When her parents took her to the hospital, the doctors first thought she was suffering from a tumor. The father of the baby is unknown.

Fact 203: Bodies transported by an airplane are denoted by "HUGO" for "Human Gone".

Fact 204: Living in the White House is not for free for the President of the United States. He receives a monthly bill for food and other expenses.

Fact 205: Because of pressure balance it is impossible to whistle in a space suit.

Fact 206: In Stockholm Sweden, there is a pilot project, which involves receiving an SMS when someone has a heart attack nearby and the ambulance has been called. Then the receiver can rush to the location and execute a heart lung massage. So far 9,500 people have joined this project and in 54 percent of the cases, people reach the location before the ambulance and were able to provide assistance.

Fact 207: The cousins of Sailor Moon are Sailor Uranus and Sailor Neptune.

Fact 208: The first name of Master Yoda from Star Wars is "Minch".

Fact 209: Golf balls were originally made of wood.

Fact 210: Helium is the only element that was not first discovered on Earth. Instead, it was discovered in 1868 in the form of previously unknown spectral lines in the light of the sun.

Fact 211: Scientist Maurice R. Hilleman developed a total of 40 different vaccines during his lifetime. Among the most important ones are vaccines against measles, mumps, chickenpox, rubella, hepatitis A and B, pneumonia and meningitis.

Fact 212: A normal person can distinguish up to one million colors. Approximately three percent of the female population can, however, perceive over 100 million different colors due to an additional photoreceptor in the eye.

Fact 213: As the earth rotates slower around the sun from year to year, 2016 was one second longer than 2015.

Fact 214: Sony earns more money as an insurance company than by selling electronics.

Fact 215: Peanuts are not nuts but in fact beans.

Fact 216: The glass globe above the German Reichstag building symbolizes that politics should always be transparent and that the people stand over the government.

Fact 217: Although the Incas had a huge empire, they did not possess money. The inhabitants paid their taxes in the form of man power and got food in exchange for this.

Fact 218: The Bluetooth logo is composed of the old Nordic runes for H and B, which were the initials of Viking king Harald Bluetooth. He was known for his overwhelming communication skills.

Fact 219: The Norwegian Lundehund is the only type of dog with six toes per paw.

Fact 220: In Finland every traffic ticket is based on your personal income. The highest fine ever paid for speeding was 100,000 Euros.

Fact 221: Blue whales are the heaviest animals in the history of the earth. With a length of up to 110 feet, they weigh a total of 150 tons.

Fact 222: Anna Kopchovsky, the first woman to cycle around the world in 1894, had only learned how to cycle a few days before she set off. She covered the entire distance in 15 months and received a reward of 10,000 dollars.

Fact 223: The Bonobo Kanzi monkey is able to make its own bonfire and cook its food in it.

Fact 224: Traffic in central London moves at just 10 miles per hour which is the same speed as a horse runs.

Fact 225: In 2014, Englishman Rory Curtis woke from a coma and thought he was the actor Matthew McConaughey.

Fact 226: Studies show that doctors who play video games perform surgical procedures more precisely than other doctors.

Fact 227: Central Park in New York is larger than the State Monaco.

Fact 228: Some cities in the United States have started spraying Christmas trees still standing in the woods in winter with fox urine. It is odorless while frozen, but smells awful as soon as it melts. This is to prevent tree thieves from going into the forest to cut down a Christmas tree on their own.

Fact 229: Panama is the only country in the world in which the sun rises above the Pacific Ocean and sets over the Atlantic Ocean.

Fact 230: Schools test only your memory and not your intelligence.

Fact 231: The Huntsman spider (Heteropoda maxima) is the largest spider species in the world. Adult males usually have a span of up to 12 inches. In Australia, a specimen estimated at 15.7 inches was discovered in 2017.

Fact 232: Rock Bottom Remainders is a music band in which Simpsons creator Matt Groening and book author Stephen King are members.

Fact 233: The skin region between a person's eyebrows is called "glabella".

Fact 234: The Hercules beetle and the Titan beetle are the two largest known beetle species. Both grow to a length of up to 6.7 inches.

Fact 235: "Banzai Skydiving" is an extreme sport where a parachutist first throws his parachute out of the plane and then jumps after it.

Fact 236: The skin that snakes leave behind during moulting is called a "snake shirt".

Fact 237: It takes the sun 226 million years to circumnavigate the Milky Way.

Fact 238: When Hitler visited Paris during World War Two, activists cut the elevator cables of the Eifel Tower so that he had to climb the stairs all the way to the top.

Fact 239: Canada has more lakes than any other country in the world.

Fact 240: A study showed that the sight of meat has a soothing effect on men.

Fact 241: In France it is not prohibited to marry a dead person.

Fact 242: Although Alexander Fleming discovered penicillin, he never developed an antibiotic from it. It was not until decades later that Howard Florey discovered Fleming's little-noticed scientific paper and recognized the potential of this discovery.

Fact 243: Walnuts contain just as much protein as eggs.

Fact 244: In 1983 Marvel released a comic series called "Spider-Pig". The main character was "Peter Porker".

Fact 245: Iceland has the lowest population density in the EU - only 9.1 people per square mile.

Fact 246: The real name of the Michelin mascot is "Bibendum" or "Bib" for short.

Fact 247: From a scientific point of view, eight days is the optimal length for a holiday. Longer holidays do not bring more happiness. Instead, it is recommended to take several short holidays.

Fact 248: The first part of the horror film series "Paranormal Activity" only had a production budget of 15,000 dollars, but went on to take in over 194 million dollars at the box office.

Fact 249: If you dissolve Viagra in water and give it to your plants, they remain fresh up to a week longer.

Fact 250: In 1923, a dead rider finished first in a horse race in New York. The rider suffered a heart attack during the race and the horse carried the dead body to the finishing line.

Fact 251: Bruce Lee was a gifted dancer. He won the Cha-Cha Championship in Hong Kong in 1958.

Fact 252: You need at least 17 given numbers in a Sudoku to ensure there is a single, unambiguous solution.

Fact 253: Black panthers are not an actual species. Instead, these are really leopards or jaguars that due to a genetic defect have a black coat.

Fact 254: To date, it is not clear why people and other animals need sleep. There are many theories, but even experts are uncertain about their accuracy.

Fact 255: While the Atlantic grows by a few inches every year, the Pacific Ocean is shrinking.

Fact 256: A cheetah can briefly reach speeds of up to 75 miles per hour. However, the sprint exhausts it so much that it needs between 20 and 60 minutes to recuperate before eating. Other predators therefore often try to steal its food in the meantime.

Fact 257: The name "Google" is derived from the word "googol" which denotes a one followed by one hundred zeros.

Fact 258: In addition to the domain google.com or google.de, Google also owns all the domains that users typically enter when they mistype: gogle.com, gooogle.com, googlr.com. The numbered variant 466453.com also belongs to the search engine company.

Fact 259: Gary Numan is older than Gary Oldman.

Fact 260: There is a disease in which boys are born with testicles, but these remain inside the body after birth. The child's penis is also so underdeveloped that the genitals resemble a vagina. Regular male genitals do not develop until puberty. 90 percent of all those affected live in the Dominican Republic, where the disease is also known as "Guevedoces", which roughly translates as "balls at twelve".

Fact 261: In India there are milkshakes with marijuana.

Fact 262: 25% of all languages in the world are spoken only in Africa. In total there are more than 2,000 different languages recognized on the continent.

Fact 263: The record for most passengers on an airplane was set in 1991 with 1,081 people. Two babies were born during the flight.

Fact 264: People in Norway who own electric cars, are allowed to park everywhere for free, do not have to pay for the ferryboat and can drive in the bus lane.

Fact 265: In the United States at least one person per hour gets killed in a car accident due to drinking.

Fact 266: On average, left-handers live longer than right-handers.

Fact 267: Without bats, there would be no tequila, as bats play a crucial role in pollinating agave plants, from which the alcohol is won.

Fact 268: The two oldest cats in the world reached an age of 34 and 38. Both belonged to the same owner. She exclusively fed her cats bacon, eggs, broccoli and coffee.

Fact 269: Lynlee Hope Boemer was born twice. In the 23rd week of pregnancy, the girl was taken out of her mother's womb by doctors to remove a tumor. After the successful operation, the girl was placed back into the womb, and twelve weeks later the healthy baby was born.

Fact 270: In 2010 a professor at the Kansas State University wanted to show his students that during a diet only the amount of calories is important, and not the nutrients. For two months he almost exclusively ate candy and lost more than 26 pounds.

Fact 271: In 1998, Marvel offered Sony the film rights for all its superheroes for only 25 million dollars. Sony rejected the deal, however, and only bought the rights to Spider Man for ten million dollars, believing that the viewers would only be interested in this character.

Fact 272: Penguins have an organ above their eyes that can convert seawater into fresh water.

Fact 273: Only eight percent of the world's money is physical. The rest exists digitally.

Fact 274: The earth is the only planet in our solar system, that is not named after a god.

Fact 275: In Pittsburgh there is a restaurant called "Conflict Kitchen". It only serves dishes from countries the USA is in conflict with. When the restaurant started to serve dishes from Palestine the owners received death threats.

Fact 276: Until the end of the 19th century, there were so-called quaggas living in the world. Although this was not a cross between a horse and a zebra, the animals were striped in the front like zebras, while the trunk was evenly reddish-brown, therefore more closely resembling a horse. Since a quagga was a subspecies of the plains zebra, South African researchers have been trying for many years to revive the breed - and their efforts have now been crowned with success.

Fact 277: Qizai is the name of the only brown panda bear in the world. Its brown coat color is due to a genetic mutation.

Fact 278: Until the 20th century, Ugandans could still pay with the shell of a cowrie snail. At the height of the currency's strength, you could buy a woman for two snails.

Fact 279: Italian Frank Lentini was born in 1889 with three legs, four feet, 16 toes and two genital organs. Until his death he earned his living as a circus artist.

Fact 280: Throughout its career, the British rock band Pink Floyd has released so many songs with astronomical allusions that scientists have named an asteroid after the band. "19367 Pink Floyd" was discovered in 1997 and has a diameter of over 4,100 miles.

Fact 281: If you start counting from one, then 1,000 is the first number in which the letter "A" occurs.

Fact 282: During the volcanic eruption of 1902 in Saint-Pierre all inhabitants of the city died. Only one man who was held as a prisoner outside the city survived.

Fact 283: The construction of the Titanic cost seven million dollars. The film starring Leonardo DiCaprio cost 200 million dollars to produce.

Fact 284: "Lifetime" paid 750,000 dollars per episode for the worldwide distribution rights on the TV show "How I Met Your Mother".

Fact 285: You can watch a 360-degree view of the Mount Everest base camp in Google Street View.

Fact 286: Besides Steve Jobs and Steve Wozniak there was a third founder of Apple: Roland Wayne. He sold his shares in 1976 for 800 dollars.

Fact 287: The actress Mila Kunis suffers from heterochromia iridum. So she has two different eye colors.

Fact 288: In 2000, Michael Jackson was included in the Guinness Book of World Records as the most philanthropic musician of all time. During his career he donated more than 300 million dollars, and during his tours he visited hospitals and orphanages to give presents to the children.

Fact 289: In 2015, the Italian city of Collecchio passed a law that only allowed the use of silent fireworks. The objective of this is to reduce stress on animals and children. Since then, many other European cities have followed this example.

Fact 290: Scientists assume that 10,000 years ago all humans still had brown eyes. It was only around this time that the first people with blue eyes were born in the region around the Black Sea. This is seen as an indication that humans continue to develop in their evolutionary biology.

Fact 291: On average, each major character of "How I Met Your Mother" earned 120,000 dollars per episode. Barney Stinson actor Neil Patrick Harris earned 210,000 dollars per episode.

Fact 292: NASA wants to send a probe to Uranus within the next 15 years.

Fact 293: After Steve Jobs' secretary was late due to her car breaking down, he later that afternoon gave her the keys to a new Jaguar, and told her, "Here, don't be late anymore."

Fact 294: The "Big Ben" has its own Twitter account with 450,000 followers. Every hour a new tweet with "Bong, Bong, Bong" appears, whereby the number of "bongs" varies with the hour.

Fact 295: The oldest bar in Ireland, which still exists, was opened 900 years before Christ.

Fact 296: If all the gold in the world was melted, a dice with an edge length of 66 feet would be the result.

Fact 297: Ruby Bridges was the first black child to attend a whites-only school in the southern United States. Most of the teachers at the New Orleans school refused to teach the girl, and some parents forbid their children to make contact with their new schoolmate. Ruby and her family received death threats over and over again, so she initially had to be escorted to school by at least three police officers.

Fact 298: Death from being overworked and work-related stress are such a common cause of death in Japan that the Japanese even have their own word for it: Karōshi.

Fact 299: The largest shark that ever lived was the Megalodon. It could grow to a length of up to 65 feet, almost three times the size of a white shark.

Fact 300: The 2022 World Soccer Championship will be opened in Lusail (Qatar), a city which did not exist till recently.

Fact 301: Bushes and clouds in Super Mario Bros have the same shape, only the color is different.

Fact 302: After the shooting of the first part of "Planet of the Apes" in 1968, actors and producers unanimously reported that a phenomenon of self-imposed "racial segregation" occurred during lunch breaks. The actors preferred to stay with their "fellow species" in the same costume instead of mixing randomly or spending time with their usual friends.

Fact 303: The sandbox tree has sharp tips on its bark which are poisonous. The tree's fruits explode at a speed of up to 155 miles per hour when they are ripe.

Fact 304: The sign on the entrance of the town Kurt Cobain was born in, reads "Come as you are".

Fact 305: Einstein believed that mankind would only survive four years after the extinction of bees.

Fact 306: It has been scientifically proven that yawning is more contagious in winter than in summer.

Fact 307: Sony has developed a refrigerator which exclusively is opened while smiling.

Fact 308: On average a spacesuit costs eleven million dollars.

Fact 309: When donating blood, the human body burns an additional 650 calories.

Fact 310: To keep up with speedsters, the police of Dubai are equipped with Ferraris and Lamborghinis.

Fact 311: The Amazon logo is the company's name and a smile that goes from A to Z. This is to express the idea that anything is sent to anyone anywhere in the world.

Fact 312: Amazon was originally supposed to be called "Cadabra". But when the founder's lawyer understood "cadaver", a different name was chosen.

Fact 313: Katherine Johnson, an African American born in 1918, was an incredible mathematician. Due to her special abilities, she attended high school at the age of ten and completed her studies when she was only 18. When she later worked for NASA, her talent for math was soon recognized and it became her job to verify the accuracy of computer-calculated orbits for planets.

Fact 314: The majority of Canada's population lives south of Seattle.

Fact 315: If you watch all Saw movies at once, it will take you 666 minutes.

Fact 316: People with blue eyes have a higher tolerance threshold for alcohol and are therefore drunk only after consuming larger quantities of alcohol.

Fact 317: Nutella has a sun protection factor of 9.5.

Fact 318: In India, 45 percent of all residents have a mobile phone, but only 30 percent have access to a toilet.

Fact 319: It takes about 100,000 years for the sun's energy to penetrate out from the core of the sun to the outermost layer and only eight minutes until it reaches the earth.

Fact 320: It is estimated that about 220,000 marriage proposals are made each year on Valentine's Day.

Fact 321: The deepest hole ever explored by man was 7.5 miles deep. Compared to that, the earth has a diameter of 7,926 miles.

Fact 322: Wildlife goldfishes can live up to 40 years.

Fact 323: In Finland, people love crazy sports. There are world championships in swamp football, mosquito catching and mobile phone throwing.

Fact 324: Sean Connery was wearing a hairpiece for all his James Bond movies because he already began balding at the age of 21.

Fact 325: Ben Affleck was banned for life from playing at Hard Rock Casino in Las Vegas after security caught him counting cards while playing Blackjack.

Fact 326: Only two percent of the world's population is blonde from birth.

Fact 327: When Amazon's website was unavailable for 49 minutes in 2013, the company lost $5.7 million in revenue.

Fact 328: Although Clint Eastwood smokes in almost all of his movies, he himself is not a smoker.

Fact 329: The Islamic movement "Moro Islamic Liberation Front" calls itself "MILF".

Fact 330: Unlike other cats of prey, the snow leopard is not aggressive towards humans. To this day, there has not been a single known case in which a snow leopard attacked a human.

Fact 331: With a diameter of up to 6.6 feet and a length of up to 120 feet, the lion's mane jellyfish is the largest jellyfish in the world. It is even longer than a blue whale.

Fact 332: When the first telephones came people answered their call with "ahoy".

Fact 333: Since 2010, Google has bought on average one company a week.

Fact 334: An interesting new pattern of behavior was observed in Japanese crows. Nuts, which the animals are not able to crack on their own, are increasingly thrown onto roads by the crows so that cars drive over them and crack them. Afterwards, the crow flies back to the open nut and collects the contents.

Fact 335: An average Facebook user has 342 friends.

Fact 336: The former U.S. politician Thomas Jefferson believed that every law should automatically become void after 19 years, to be replaced by a new law, which is adjusted to the new generation.

Fact 337: The largest Bolivian prison, San Pedro in La Paz, has developed its own society. There are no guards in the prison, and the prisoners organize all aspects of their lives themselves. There are shops and restaurants run by the prisoners, and at regular intervals the inmates even elect a new leader.

Fact 338: The Paricutín volcano in Mexico was not there until 20 February 1943. Witnesses report having worked on a maize field that day and heard a dull "plop". A day later, the volcano was already 33 feet high, and by the next day it had grown to 164 feet. A year later, the volcano had reached a height of 1,102 feet when it began to spew lava. Today, the volcano is 1,391 feet high and continues to be active.

Fact 339: Ring announcer Michael Buffer had his famous phrase "Let's get ready to rumble" trademarked back in 1992. To date, this has earned him more than 400 million dollars.

Fact 340: Up until his death, F. Scott Fitzgerald was convinced that he had achieved nothing in his life. Two years later, his book "The Great Gatsby" was sent to soldiers in World War II and became an immediate success. To this day, the book sells about 500,000 copies every year.

Fact 341: The first seven seconds are the most important when making a first impression.

Fact 342: Approximately 96 percent of all French secondary schools have condom vending machines on their grounds.

Fact 343: Because it was impossible to transport the ingredients needed for Coca Cola to Nazi Germany, the Coca Cola Company designed a beverage especially for the German market: Fanta.

Fact 344: "Nomophobia" describes the fear of not being available via mobile phone.

Fact 345: In London the buses are red because the owner wanted to stand out from the competitors.

Fact 346: A study has shown that four percent of all people dream exclusively in black-and-white.

Fact 347: The Foreign Accent Syndrome describes a disease in which the affected persons involuntarily speak their mother tongue with a foreign accent.

Fact 348: The Kennedy Space Center in Cape Canaveral is located at exactly 28 degrees north latitude, as the moon's orbit is also rotated by 28 degrees relative to the equator. When flying to the moon, you therefore receive maximum momentum from the earth's rotation.

Fact 349: The longest street in the world connects Alaska with the south of Argentina. It has a length of approximately 18,641 miles and crosses 17 states, six time zones and four climate zones.

Fact 350: While tomatoes are typically classified as vegetables, they actually belong to the fruit category.

Fact 351: The cactus "Saguaro" can grow up to 20 feet tall and live for over 300 years.

Fact 352: The Christmas tree that is set up every year on London's Trafalgar Square is always given to the British by Norway. This tradition has existed since 1947 and is intended to express the Norwegians' gratitude for the support by the British during the Second World War.

Fact 353: Nintendo originally did not develop consoles and video games, but rather started off producing playing cards.

Fact 354: In northern Finland, the sun never sets from June to July - it shines all day long. In winter, however, the opposite is the case. The sun never rises and the sky is at best only bathed in a dark blue.

Fact 355: In 2009, Marc Aurus - an expert on the prevention of kidnapping - gave a lecture on the topic of "How to avoid being kidnapped in Mexico" and was then kidnapped.

Fact 356: City birds are now integrating cigarette stubs into their nests as they have recognized that these are effective against insects.

Fact 357: The honor code of comic book authors forbids the use of werewolves in comics.

Fact 358: Jim Cummings, the voice of Winnie Pooh in the U.S., regularly calls seriously ill children in hospitals and talks to them in his Winnie Pooh voice to delight them.

Fact 359: When Great Britain returned Hong Kong to China in 1997 after years of colonization, it was agreed that Hong Kong should continue as a democratic state with its own laws, its own economy and its own currency. However, this agreement will expire in 2047 and China will take full control of Hong Kong from then on.

Fact 360: Gladiators in ancient Rome were exclusively fighters who fought against other humans for life and death. People fighting exclusively against animals were called "Bestiarii".

Fact 361: Scientist Max Planck was advised by his professor Philipp von Jolly not to go into physics, as almost everything had already been discovered in theoretical physics. Planck replied that he only wanted to learn the basics. In 1919, Planck was awarded the Nobel Prize for his development of quantum theory.

Fact 362: Defenestration is the term used to describe a person falling out of a window.

Fact 363: The production cost of one penny is 1.7 cents.

Fact 364: According to scientists, the giant tortoise Jonathan was born around 1832 in the Seychelles and is therefore the oldest living reptile on earth. Some researchers even believe that Jonathan may be the oldest living land animal.

Fact 365: The place with the lowest gravitational pull is in Canada.

Fact 366: On 13 February 2019, NASA officially lost contact with its Mars rover "Opportunity". Originally, the rover was planned to be used for only 90 days, but instead it would continue to send data to Earth for more than 15 years. Contact was ultimately lost when the rover got caught in a sandstorm.

Fact 367: There are no mosquitoes in Iceland. Scientists are not sure why this is the case, but it is suspected that the special weather conditions of Iceland have something to do with the phenomenon.

Fact 368: In the U.S. state of Minnesota, a three-year-old was mayor for a short time.

Fact 369: Netflix has existed longer than Google.

Fact 370: The first dinosaur bones were not discovered and scientifically described until 1824. So before that, people never knew that dinosaurs used to roam our planet.

Fact 371: On average, a raindrop reaches a speed of 21.7 miles per hour.

Fact 372: In the Trevi Fountain in Rome 3,000 Euros is thrown in by tourists every day.

Fact 373: The mountain range "Witwatersrand" in South Africa is source of half the gold ever mined on Earth.

Fact 374: Mosquitoes have killed more people than any other animal. It is estimated that mosquitoes kill more people worldwide in five minutes than sharks do in a whole year.

Fact 375: In France it is prohibited by law, to name a pig "Napoleon".

Fact 376: Because of a reduction in the emission of greenhouse gases, scientists predict that the ozone hole will close in 2075.

Fact 377: A person has between 100,000 and 150,000 hairs on their head.

Fact 378: The Audi brand name e-tron means "pile of shit" in French.

Fact 379: The Nile crocodile is the world's largest reptile and can only be found in Africa.

Fact 380: Current research assumes that Jesus was not born on 25 December, but rather in March. So instead of commemorating Jesus Christ at Christmas, we should instead honor Isaac Newton, who was verifiably born on 25 December.

Fact 381: Termite queens have the longest life expectancy of all insects. They can live up to 50 years.

Fact 382: In 1949 a boxing match was held between boxer Gus Waldorf and a bear. The bear was given a muzzle and boxing gloves to create "fair" conditions for both fighters. In the end, however, it was the bear that won.

Fact 383: Walt Disney has received 63 Oscar nominations throughout his lifetime, of which he has won 26. Thus, he is the world record holder of most Oscar wins.

Fact 384: google.com is the only website that maintains that users should spend as little time on it as possible.

Fact 385: In 1856 a man from Havana took off in his hot air balloon and was never seen again.

Fact 386: Samuel L. Jackson as Nick Fury is the actor who has most often played the same role in a comic book adaptation. Second place goes to Hugh Jackman as Wolverine.

Fact 387: In Stockholm, Sweden, there is speed camera which raffles the income from speeding tickets among those who drive at the correct speed.

Fact 388: Worms, officially the oldest city in Germany, was inhabited as early as 5,000 BC.

Fact 389: Mikhail Kalashnikov, the inventor of the AK-47 assault rifle, today regrets having built the weapon. In retrospect, he wishes he had invented something that had benefitted mankind, such as a lawnmower, for example.

Fact 390: With an IQ of approximately 230, the Australian mathematician Terence Tao is the most intelligent person in the world.

Fact 391: The westernmost point of the USA and the easternmost point of Russia lie just three miles apart.

Fact 392: The world's largest vegetables grow in Alaska. The main reason for this is that in summer the sun shines for more than 20 hours a day.

Fact 393: Laurence Tureaud, better known by his pseudonym "Mr. T", chose this stage name because his father, uncle and brother had always been called "boy" by everyone. He believed that black people deserved more respect and therefore always wanted to be called "Mister".

Fact 394: When Michael Jackson died in 2009, this caused several websites, including Twitter and Wikipedia, to crash, as many people wanted to know more about his death and overloaded the website operators' servers.

Fact 395: Frequent sex increases the growth of brain cells.

Fact 396: In 2005 and 2007, graffiti artist David Choe painted several works of art in Facebook's offices. Instead of cash, however, he was paid with Facebook shares, which were worth over $200 million when the company went public.

Fact 397: Just five percent of all babies suck their left thumb. The remaining 95 percent use their right one.

Fact 398: The starting melody of Windows was composed on a Mac.

Fact 399: During "How I Met Your Mother" there have been 13 interventions. The most popular ones were Barneys frequent usage of magic tricks, Marshals addiction to charts and Lilly's fake British accent.

Fact 400: Vin Diesel invested 3,000 dollars to produce the film "Multi Facial". The film was about his problems getting a real major role. Steven Spielberg watched the movie and cast Vin Diesel for his first major role in "The Soldier James Ryan". From then on his career began.

Fact 401: Since 2013, every citizen of Uruguay is allowed to buy 40 grams of marijuana at a pharmacy for their own personal use. Due to the good price of one dollar per gram, as specified by the state, many former drug lords have left the now unprofitable drug business.

Fact 402: The manchineel tree is so poisonous that even rainwater trickling off the fruit can lead to severe acid burns to the skin. If you get smoke in your eyes while burning the tree, you might go blind. It is even recommended to not inhale too much air around the tree as even this can cause dizziness and nausea.

Fact 403: An octopus has its brain in its tentacles. Even if the tentacles are separated from the body, they continue to search for food for a short time and bring them to a mouth which is no longer present.

Fact 404: The earthquake that struck Japan in 2011 with a magnitude of 9.0 was so strong that it changed the earth's mass. Since then, one day on earth has been 1.8 microseconds shorter.

Fact 405: During World War II, the Nazis attempted to cover the river Alster as part of their "Operation Cloak of Invisibility". They covered parts of the river with wood and wire, built dummy houses and planted trees on the frozen river, as they suspected that the Allies were using the Alster for orientation. The objective was to save Hamburg's city center from more severe bomb damage. However, this hope was not fulfilled.

Fact 406: McDonald's is not the largest restaurant chain in the world. Subway is.

Fact 407: The reflex that we automatically lead a small wound to our mouth is an innate protective mechanism. The saliva in our mouth helps the blood to coagulate and kills bacteria.

Fact 408: The day-night boundary, i.e. the boundary that separates the side of the earth exposed to sunlight from the unexposed shadow side, is also called the "terminator".

Fact 409: The London Underground now makes more profit by selling its popular underground maps than it does operating the subway.

Fact 410: If you could drive directly to the moon by car at a speed of 80 miles per hour, it would take about four months to reach it.

Fact 411: The very first .com domain, symbolics.com, was registered on 15 March 1985.

Fact 412: 2013 became the first year after 1987 not to contain a repeating digit.

Fact 413: In order to die of a caffeine overdose, a person would have to consume about 100 cups of coffee in a very short time.

Fact 414: The more educated a couple is, the lower the probability of divorce.

Fact 415: An average, one U.S. citizen consumes as many resources per day as 32 people in Kenya.

Fact 416: The English term "Goodbye" is a shortening of the religious phrase "God be with ye" that has developed over time.

Fact 417: In the Simpsons, God and Jesus are the only characters with five fingers.

Fact 418: A substitute for cling film made of crab shells and plant fibers was developed in the United States.

Fact 419: In biological terms, love is an addiction. The serotonin level among lovers is as low as among drug dependents.

Fact 420: In 1783, the volcano Lakagígar in the south of Iceland erupted. For months, lava erupted from over 100 craters. Numerous aerosols such as carbon monoxide, carbon dioxide and sulphur were blown into the atmosphere and began to darken the sky over all of Europe. Crop failures and the mass death of livestock led to a famine that cost the lives of about 10,000 people. Even the famine that struck France in 1788, which together with the high tax burden at the time led to the French Revolution, could have been a consequence of the volcanic eruption.

Fact 421: The term "soap opera" can be traced back to the US company Procter & Gamble. In the 1930s, the detergent manufacturer produced a daily radio broadcast for women with a simple plot for advertising purposes, which soon became known as the soap opera.

Fact 422: For his role as Harry Potter, actor Daniel Radcliffe received a total pay of 74 million pounds. According to his own account, the actor has spent almost none of the money so far.

Fact 423: Due to their fine and extensive root network, forest mushrooms absorb heavy metals in large quantities. That is why you should not eat more than 250 grams of forest mushrooms per week.

Fact 424: The word "Flubber" is a portmanteau word composed of the two words "flying rubber". In German, there is a similar term "Flummy", made up of the German words for "flying rubber" (fliegender Gummi), which refers to a bouncy ball.

Fact 425: Originally, Grand Theft Auto was meant to be a racing game named "Race'n'Chase" but a glitch made police cars ram into the car of the player. This element was so popular with the game testers that a whole game was modelled on this principle and GTA was born.

Fact 426: Since 1987 Starbucks on average opens two stores a day.

Fact 427: The planet Uranus was discovered in 1781, while the Antarctic was not discovered until 1820.

Fact 428: The least people are born in February.

Fact 429: Approximately one in 5,000 babies is born without an anus due to a deformity. Doctors then need to artificially reconstruct it after birth.

Fact 430: If you salt a pineapple, it tastes sweeter.

Fact 431: Every year, about four million cats are consumed as delicacies in China.

Fact 432: McDonald's earns 8.7 billion dollars a year though franchise revenue only. That is more than the gross domestic product of Mongolia.

Fact 433: There is no physical description of Jesus in the Bible.

Fact 434: "Hot Neptune" is the name given to a planet in which temperatures of more than 10,800 degrees Fahrenheit prevail, but which due to extremely high air pressure nevertheless consists of solid ice.

Fact 435: Because the movie "Psycho" was produced in black-and-white, chocolate syrup was used for blood.

Fact 436: In 1990, the Michigan police organized a wedding of two of their undercover agents. Numerous drug dealers have been invited and were arrested during the wedding ceremony.

Fact 437: Most "Converse" sneakers have a small piece of felt on the sole, which usually comes off after wearing the shoe for the first time. The reason for this is that due to the piece of felt, the shoes are officially categorized as house shoes and therefore carry lower import duties.

Fact 438: Most books stolen in German universities are legal books. The second most commonly stolen books are books with a theological background.

Fact 439: First chimpanzee conspecifics now use stones as tools, for example to crack open fruit. Therefore, the Stone Age has officially begun for chimpanzees.

Fact 440: In Austria there are three toilets, which are listed for preservation.

Fact 441: "K'o K'ou K'o Lê", the phonetically correct Chinese translation for Coca-Cola, literally means "A female horse fastened with wax".

Fact 442: Brazilian natives used ants as wound clamps. They let the ants bite and close the wound with their pincers and then pulled off their bodies. The pincers remained wedged in the body, closing the wound.

Fact 443: Serbian flight attendant Vesna Vulović holds the world record for the highest fall a person has ever survived without a parachute. In 1972, an explosion occurred on an airplane, causing her to fall from a height of more than six miles. She was also the only person to survive the flight.

Fact 444: "Mr. Bean" actor Rowan Atkinson holds a master's degree in electrical engineering.

Fact 445: According to current estimates, it would cost more than 23 billion dollars to build a real "Jurassic Park".

Fact 446: Because of their extremely hairy chest the "Hasselhoff crab" was named after David Hasselhoff.

Fact 447: In a kidney transplant, the non-functional kidney is usually not removed from the body. Instead, the new donor kidney is inserted into the groin, meaning that after a kidney transplant, the patient has three kidneys.

Fact 448: The longest sentence in a book can be found in "Les Miserable". It consists of 823 words.

Fact 449: Jabbar Collins was imprisoned for 16 years. During this time he read numerous law books and found a procedural error which led to his freedom and a compensation of ten million dollars.

Fact 450: Bolivia has a 1,800-man naval unit, although the country has no access to the open sea at all.

Fact 451: Worms can have up to ten hearts.

Fact 452: Babies are not able to taste salt until they are four months old.

Fact 453: It is impossible to move your eyes smoothly from left to right or vice versa without interruption, unless you are following a moving object. The reason for this is that the eye always jumps from focus point to focus point with every movement.

Fact 454: Chia seeds contain five times more calcium than milk and twice as much iron as spinach.

Fact 455: People with creative professions have higher life expectancies than people with other professions.

Fact 456: Michael Jackson proposed a Harry Potter musical, but J. K. Rowling refused.

Fact 457: Benjamin Franklin left the cities of Boston and Philadelphia 2,000 dollars each in his will, with the instruction that the money could not be touched for 200 years. Due to inflation and clever investments, the two cities ended up receiving 6.5 million dollars in 1990.

Fact 458: There is more bacteria on your own skin then there are living people in the world.

Fact 459: Scientist Nikola Tesla once paid a hotel bill with the first functional model of his "death ray". Management was advised not to open the box unless complying with strict safety precautions. After his death, the box was opened, and it turned out to contain nothing but old laboratory utensils.

Fact 460: Popeye has four nephews named Pupeye, Pipeye, Peepeye and Poopeye.

Fact 461: The often mentioned "Bro Code" and "Playbook" are real books, which can be bought.

Fact 462: Around 35 percent of all billionaires have never graduated from a university.

Fact 463: Men more frequently dream of other men, while women dream of both sexes equally.

Fact 464: In September 1944, nine US pilots set off to fly a maneuver against the Japanese. However, all nine planes were shot down by Japanese troops, and eight of the pilots were captured, beaten, tortured and beheaded and had parts of their bodies eaten by the Japanese soldiers. The ninth pilot who escaped was George H. W. Bush who would later go on to become the President of the United States.

Fact 465: Behind Lincoln's face in Mount Rushmore, there is a secret chamber where memorabilia of the most important historical events in the USA are kept. The room is not accessible to tourists.

Fact 466: A building is considered a skyscraper if it is at least 492 feet high.

Fact 467: Strawberries are not berries, but in fact nuts.

Fact 468: In Estonia, Wi-Fi is made freely available to all citizens - even to the 90 percent who live in the forests.

Fact 469: The first hard disk for Apple II had a capacity of five megabyte.

Fact 470: Each year around 1,000 people die because they are struck by lightning.

Fact 471: From 1409 to 1417, there were three different popes, all claiming to be the head of the Catholic Church.

Fact 472: A study has shown that the brain can remember things on paper more easily than their digital equivalent.

Fact 473: Coca-Cola owns the websites ahh.com, ahhh.com and so on. The website with the longest URL contains 62 "h"s.

Fact 474: After Google installed the "Did you mean" function in its search engine, the number of search queries doubled almost overnight.

Fact 475: 90 percent of people start fake laughing when they do not understand what others have said.

Fact 476: A study from 2003 came to the conclusion that French people, among all nations, have the most frequent sex.

Fact 477: Most accidents at work happen on Mondays.

Fact 478: The brain of an ostrich is smaller than its eyes.

Fact 479: On Friday, April 18, 1930, the news channel BBC announced in its daily program that "There is no news", because simply nothing important had happened. Instead of a news show, piano music was played for 15 minutes.

Fact 480: After the last Bucardo - a special type of wild goat - had died, scientists succeeded in creating a clone of the animal in 2003, making it the first species ever to be resurrected after its extinction. However, the clone died after only seven minutes, making it also the first species to go extinct twice.

Fact 481: James Fixx, the creator of the word "jogging" died from a heart attack while jogging.

Fact 482: There are only five people worldwide who are allowed to build the Nissan GT-R engines. They are also called "Takumi" and they are the reason why only 1,000 cars of this make can be produced per month.

Fact 483: In 1995, Newsweek published an article in which it expressed the opinion that the Internet would never make it. Meanwhile, this article is available on their website.

Fact 484: It is estimated that the world's oceans hold 320 billion cubic miles of water. To determine this magnitude, which is hard to estimate, the boundaries of the oceans were first measured using satellites. Subsequently, the average depth was determined, which in turn made it possible to calculate a volume.

Fact 485: In the 1880s, Charles Pickering, director of the Harvard Observatory, was constantly complaining about his male colleagues. One day he supposedly said that even his Scottish maid would be able to perform better. He decided to hire his housekeeper Williamina Fleming, who then went on to successfully lead a team for several decades, helping to classify thousands of stars. She even discovered a white dwarf and was the first human to find the Horsehead Nebula.

Fact 486: The Malaysian kissing bug uses the remains of its prey as a shield.

Fact 487: Grapes explode when you heat them in a microwave.

Fact 488: If you hold a grain of sand against the night sky, it will hide 10,000 galaxies from your eyes.

Fact 489: Scientists assume that the first human who will reach 150 years or more, has already be born.

Fact 490: Adolf Hitler was nominated for the Nobel Peace Prize in 1939.

Fact 491: The mouthwash "Listerine" was originally marketed as a clinical antiseptic and later, in distilled form, as a floor cleaner.

Fact 492: The video game industry generates higher sales than the film and music industries combined.

Fact 493: An estimated five million landmines are still buried in India.

Fact 494: Deep down in the Sala silver mine in Sweden, there is a hotel room 509 feet underground, making it the deepest hotel in the world.

Fact 495: Every year, humans kill up to 100 million sharks to get to their fins.

Fact 496: The U.S. channel Fox has the rights on the Simpsons until 2082.

Fact 497: In Texas, there is a city called Earth; it is the only place in the world named "Earth".

Fact 498: Bangladesh, although just one percent the size of Russia, is more populated.

Fact 499: The Hard Rock Cafe T-shirts are the world's best-selling T-shirts.

Fact 500: In Spain there is a comedy club in which you pay per laugh.

Fact 501: Jeanne Calment holds the world record as the longest living human being. She was the first person to verifiably live to celebrate her 116th to 122nd birthday. She was born in 1875, saw the Eiffel Tower being built, sold paint brushes to Vincent van Gogh and died in 1997 at the age of 122.

Fact 502: Dalmatian puppies are born with a white coat. The black dots only appear after a while in the course of their childhood.

Fact 503: The thermometer was invented in Italy.

Fact 504: In the evening, people are about half an inch smaller than in the morning, as the spine compresses during the day due to the effects of gravity.

Fact 505: When Mario had his first act in Donkey Kong in 1981, his name was "Jumpman".

Fact 506: Because all passports in the UK are officially issued by the Queen, she does not own a passport. When travelling abroad she just has to state that she is the Queen.

Fact 507: The concept of "rap battles" dates back to the fifth century. At that time, poets competed against each other in a public competition in which they rhymed insults and sexual perversions. This tradition was particularly popular in Nordic and Celtic cultures. There are stories about the Nordic god Loki, who insulted other gods in rhyme form, and even William Shakespeare refers to this in some of his plays.

Fact 508: Popcorn has been around since 3,600 BC.

Fact 509: One fifth of all people use their smartphone during sex.

Fact 510: The Romanian scientist Nicolas Minovici explored death by hanging and for his studies hanged himself from a gallows several times.

Fact 511: Based on statistics, the best drivers have the zodiac sign Leo while the worst drivers are Taurus.

Fact 512: It takes eight minutes and 17 seconds until the light from the sun reaches the earth.

Fact 513: A phenomenon referred to as the "CSI effect" explains when jurymen become influenced by television series such as "CSI Miami".

Fact 514: There are green birds, reptiles and insects, but no green mammals.

Fact 515: When you obtain a doctorate in Finland, you receive a hat and a sword from your university.

Fact 516: In 2005 a used pregnancy test belonging to Britney Spears was sold for more than 5,000 dollars on Ebay.

Fact 517: In order to prevent the Sahara from spreading from North Africa to the Sahel, the "Green Wall" project was launched in 2005. Today, 21 African states are participating in the project. Around 15 percent of the planned trees have so far been planted on the strip, which is 4,850 miles long and nine miles wide.

Fact 518: In its language selection, Facebook offers the language "pirate".

Fact 519: Two of the richest men in the world - Bill Gates and Warren Buffett - officially stated that they will donate 90 percent of their assets when they pass away.

Fact 520: All of our school textbooks show the solar system with the planets close enough to fit on one page. In actuality if you were to draw the solar system to scale and the earth was the size of a pea on paper Jupiter would be over 984 feet away and Pluto would be one and a half mile away. The nearest star would be 9,940 miles away on paper.

Fact 521: In 1954 Bob Hawke, the future prime minister of Australia, set the world record by drinking 2.5 liters of beer in 11 seconds.

Fact 522: The first server at Google was built from legos.

Fact 523: Before American Kim Peek died in 2009, he was able to read a complete book in less than an hour and remember every detail. He was able to reproduce the exact content of over 12,000 books and was the role model for Dustin Hoffman's character in the film "Rain Man".

Fact 524: In the U.S., a man stole several million dollars after having beaten a security system consisting of security guards, infrared sensors, motion detectors and a safe door. He was arrested when DNA traces were discovered on the remainders of a sandwich that was found in a trash can next to the crime scene.

Fact 525: The last time all living human beings were on Earth was on 2 November 2000. Since then, the International Space Station has been continuously occupied.

Fact 526: In terms of the level of medical accuracy, Scrubs is the best medical television series in the world.

Fact 527: The first car accident with fatalities happened in 1896 at a speed of less than four miles per hour.

Fact 528: Lake Karachay in Russia has been overrun with so much nuclear waste after World War II, that one hour of exposure is a lethal dose of radiation.

Fact 529: The spider species "Amaurobius Ferox" belongs to the genus of matriphages. This means that the spider female's children eat their own mother after hatching from their eggs.

Fact 530: The holes in Swiss cheese are called "eyes". A Swiss cheese without eyes is called "blind".

Fact 531: Johnny Depp always has his Jack Sparrow costume while travelling and visits children in hospitals regularly as Captain Jack Sparrow.

Fact 532: At birth, the blue-whale baby is already 23 feet long and weighs more than two tons.

Fact 533: The boxing ring is called a "ring" because it used to be round. Instead of its present form, the spectators used to stand in a circle around the fighters when the sport first became popular.

Fact 534: Pumba from "The Lion King" was the first Disney character who was allowed to fart.

Fact 535: The game "Quidditch" from the Harry Potter novels is now a recognized sport in our world, with its own leagues and even regular world championships.

Fact 536: A statistical survey conducted by Facebook shows that most couples separate two weeks before Christmas.

Fact 537: Between 1663 and 1673, Louis XIV, the King of France, sent 800 women to Canada to promote the settlement of a predominantly male French colony. The deployment of the so-called "Daughters of the King" ("filles du Roy" in French) quickly proved effective. The colony's population doubled within ten years, and it is estimated that about two thirds of all French Canadians can trace their roots back to these 800 women.

Fact 538: Tuesday was named after the Nordic god of justice "Tyr".

Fact 539: Einstein was asked what it was like to be the smartest guy in the world, he answered "I don't know, ask Nikola Tesla".

Fact 540: Because of the large amount of sugar in it, it is impossible for honey to spoil. Even in 1,000 years it would still be edible.

Fact 541: The oldest bridge in France is called "Pont Neuf". Translated it means "New Bridge".

Fact 542: The oldest tree in the world stands in the White Mountains in the US state of California and is more than 5,062 years old. However, it is not a sequoia, but rather a long-lived pine tree.

Fact 543: Fingernails grow approximately four times faster than toenails.

Fact 544: The Indonesian chicken species "Ayam Cermani" has a genetic peculiarity that results in the animals being completely black. Not only is the plumage of the animals black, but also their eyes, skin, flesh, bones, claws and blood. The dark coloration is due to a natural genetic disposition of the chicken, which results in the animal forming more color pigments than other species.

Fact 545: There was already McLobster, McSpaghetti and McPizza, on offer at McDonald's.

Fact 546: About 31 percent of Germany's surface is covered by forest.

Fact 547: The dance style "Daggering" was forbidden on Jamaican television, as it lead to numerous penis fractures during the dancing.

Fact 548: Due to earthquakes and tsunamis, Tokyo was destroyed and rebuilt on average every five years between 1608 and 1945.

Fact 549: In the case of "alien hand syndrome", the affected person has no control over one of his or her hands. The hand acts completely uncontrolled and in the worst case can even try to strangle the affected person.

Fact 550: For fun, a British couple invited the Queen to their wedding. The Queen actually came to the wedding.

Fact 551: Mae C. Jemison was the first female African-American astronaut in the history of space travel. In 1992 she flew into space with the space shuttle Endeavour.

Fact 552: At minimum, a person only needs one kidney with a capacity of at least 75 percent to survive.

Fact 553: The 15 largest ocean-going ships in the world emit more harmful sulphur oxides every year than 760 million cars. This corresponds to approximately two thirds of all vehicles registered worldwide in 2014.

Fact 554: Tsutomu Yamaguchi was working in Hiroshima when the first atomic bomb hit the city. As he was driving home to Nagasaki the second bomb hit. He is currently 90 years old and still alive.

Fact 555: A 60-year-old "Macallan Valerio Adami 1926" whiskey was auctioned in 2018 for 848,750 pounds, marking the highest price ever spent on a single bottle of whiskey.

Fact 556: In the Brazilian prison of Santa Rita do Sapucaí, inmates can ride stationary bicycles to generate electricity for the city's inhabitants. For every 24 hours of cycling, their detention time is shortened by one day.

Fact 557: The American pygmy shrew has to eat three times its own body weight every day. For this, the animal has to go hunting again every 15 to 30 minutes, as even an hour without food would lead to its death.

Fact 558: Regions of the earth where the inhabitants clearly exceed the average life expectancy of the world population are called "Blue Zones". Currently, only five Blue Zones are known worldwide. These are Okinawa (Japan), Sardinia (Italy), Nicola (Costa Rica), Ikaria (Greece) and Loma Linda (California). The reason why people there live so long is not clear.

Fact 559: Masabumi Hosono was the only Japanese passenger on the Titanic. Fortunately, he was rescued when the ship sank, but when he returned home he was portrayed as a coward by the media and other public authorities. He was accused of being a disgrace to the country for not sacrificing his life to save the lives of others.

Fact 560: Australia is home to 21 of the 25 most dangerous snakes in the world.

Fact 561: About 99,99999999999% of an atom is "nothing". If one would eliminate the empty space of all atoms from the entire human race, the remaining mass would fit in a coffee mug.

Fact 562: Michael James Massimino, an astronaut who has made several guest appearances in "The Big Bang Theory", was the first person to tweet from space.

Fact 563: The role of John McClane in "Die Hard" actually went to Arnold Schwarzenegger - however he declined the role.

Fact 564: John Lennon once received a letter from a fan telling him that his teacher was discussing Beatles lyrics in class. Lennon found this so funny that he composed the song "I Am The Walrus" to confuse the students with the lyrics.

Fact 565: Most suicides happen on Mondays.

Fact 566: Before there were trees on the earth, our planet was covered by giant mushrooms.

Fact 567: A "déjà-rêvé" is a dream déjà-vu. So this is a real event of which you believe that you have already seen in a dream.

Fact 568: Germany was the first country to implement summer time.

Fact 569: Koala bears hug trees to cool down on hot days.

Fact 570: The Christmas song "Jingle Bells" was originally written for Thanksgiving and not for Christmas.

Fact 571: Just one percent of all heart attacks is caused by sex whereas ten percent are brought about by getting up too fast.

Fact 572: On Mercury, one day - one revolution on its own axis - lasts 59 earth days.

Fact 573: In Italy on New Year's Eve, traditionally one wears red underwear to have luck for the new year.

Fact 574: In Surabaya, Indonesia, residents can also use plastic waste to pay for their bus ticket. The objective of the campaign is to reduce plastic waste in the city and at the same time get more people interested in public transport.

Fact 575: The Sơn-Đoòng cave in Vietnam is the largest cave in the world. It even contains a large rainforest, and its dimensions are so vast that even a Boeing 747 could easily fit inside. Despite its size, the cave was not discovered until 1991.

Fact 576: In Cambridge (Canada) you can pay your parking ticket by donating soft toys.

Fact 577: In Iceland, Greenland and the Antarctic there are no ants.

Fact 578: With a speed of 91 gigabits per second, NASA has the fastest internet-connection in the world.

Fact 579: If you trace your family tree back 25 generations, you will have 33,554,432 direct ancestors. Assuming no incest was involved.

Fact 580: In the 90s, 50 percent of all CDs produced were the free AOL Internet CD.

Fact 581: Redheads are less sensitive to pain and more sensitive to temperature compared to people with different hair colors.

Fact 582: London is the city with the most millionaires in the world. It is followed by New York City in second and Tokyo in third place.

Fact 583: The soldier Jack Churchill went into every battle of the Second World War carrying a sword, bagpipes and a longbow. During a mission in France, he even achieved the only confirmed kill by longbow during the Second World War. His comrades therefore nicknamed him "Mad Jack".

Fact 584: Each year about 100 million bikes are produced worldwide.

Fact 585: The PlayStation 2 was so popular that it was still in production until shortly before the launch of the PlayStation 4.

Fact 586: Animals like the zebra, gorilla, giraffe, chimpanzee, wildebeest or hippopotamus are unique to the African continent and can only be found here.

Fact 587: The South African rock hyrax is only 20 inches tall, weighs about 8.8 pounds and looks like a big guinea pig. Nevertheless, its closest relative is the elephant.

Fact 588: On each branching level, the branches of a tree are - in sum - as wide as the trunk of the tree.

Fact 589: With more than 500 kills, the Finnish soldier Simo Häyhä is the sniper with the highest number of confirmed kills in a war. He fought during the Second World War and killed mainly Soviet soldiers. The Red Army called him "The White Death".

Fact 590: The medical term for headaches due to eating too much ice-cream is sphenopalatine ganglioneuralgia.

Fact 591: In December 2013, the dating app Tinder delivered its first match in Antarctica. It was between a scientist and a visitor who were only a 45-minute helicopter flight apart.

Fact 592: When it comes to extreme heat in Melbourne, the lions in the zoo are given frozen blood.

Fact 593: There are currently more than 28 million miles of photographed roads in Google Street View available.

Fact 594: The guide dog Kirsch has an honorary master's degree because he attended all lectures together with his owner.

Fact 595: An ostrich can run a marathon in less than 60 minutes.

Fact 596: Some roads in Australia are so long that the Australian state counteracts the risk of fatigue by playing little trivia games with the drivers along the side of the road.

Fact 597: A short nap after studying helps the brain to remember the studied materials better.

Fact 598: In Greece, there are over 2,000 people who have registered as officially practicing the religion "Hellenism". This means that they believe in the ancient Greek gods like Zeus, Poseidon or Aphrodite.

Fact 599: Michael Jackson was negotiating to buy Marvel.

Fact 600: Mothers instinctively kiss their newborn baby. Through the kiss the mother takes up bacteria and viruses of the child and forms antibodies which can pass through the mother's milk to the child.

Fact 601: The longest "word" in the English language is the chemically correct designation of the protein "titin". Titin is only the short form of the scientific name, which correctly begins with "Methionyl..." and ends with "...isoleucine". The scientific name, however, consists of 189,819 letters and the pronunciation would take several hours, so that scientists only use the name "titin".

Fact 602: On average, a man gets eleven erections per day. Nine during his sleep.

Fact 603: There is no law in Denmark which prohibits breaking out of jail.

Fact 604: The average depth of the oceans is 2.5 miles.

Fact 605: Among the 30 fastest 100-meter sprints in the history of the sport, there are only nine that are not related to doping. All nine runs were completed by Usain Bolt.

Fact 606: In the Spanish dubbed version of "Terminator 2", the terminator does not say "Hasta la vista, baby", but "Sayonara, baby".

Fact 607: At the geographically most northern point on earth, every line you draw points south.

Fact 608: Due to plate tectonic movements, Australia migrates to the north by about 2.8 inches each year.

Fact 609: The German term "Bombenwetter" (literally: "bomb weather") can be traced back to the fact that this weather offers ideal conditions to make out targets when bombing a city. The word originated during the Second World War.

Fact 610: If Coca Cola was served without colorants, it would be green and not black.

Fact 611: Radivoje Lajic's house has been hit by a meteorite six times. Scientists are not sure why his house seems to attract the celestial objects so strongly.

Fact 612: From 5 to 9 December 1952, a fog crept up over London and claimed the lives of about 12,000 people. When strong winds finally lifted the fog, people were shocked to find so many corpses.

Fact 613: Scientists believe that it is possible to exterminate all mosquitoes, without impacting on our global ecosystem.

Fact 614: According to Bill Gates, just a small amount of poor countries will exist in 2035.

Fact 615: Instead of "LOL" people in France say MDR for "mort de rire", which means laughing to death.

Fact 616: Bruce Banner - the Hulk's alter ego - holds seven doctorates.

Fact 617: Seen chronologically, Cleopatra was closer to the moon landing than to the construction of the pyramids.

Fact 618: In Norway, you pay half the amount of normal tax in December, to have more money for Christmas.

Fact 619: When the space probes Rosetta and Philae left the earth on March 2, 2004, there were no iPhones, Facebook existed for 27 days and nobody knew of Twitter.

Fact 620: Eggs can explode in the microwave.

Fact 621: While the mortality rate for cancer ten years ago was 215 deaths per 100,000 people, it has subsequently decreased to 172.

Fact 622: In Korea, everyone is one year old from birth and turns one year older on New Year's Day.

Fact 623: The country code of Russia is 007.

Fact 624: Women who frequently play video games have more sex than other women.

Fact 625: Of the 100 oldest people of all time, only six are male.

Fact 626: The hair above a cat's eyes is called tactile hair.

Fact 627: The first ATMs required six digits as a PIN. However, after a large number of users could not remember six digits, the PIN was reduced to four digits.

Fact 628: No mammal can dive deeper than Cuvier's beaked whale. A dive into the depth of the oceans can last up to 140 minutes and, according to measurements, reach a depth of 9,816 feet.

Fact 629: The Centennial Light is the longest-lasting light bulb in the world. It has been on since 1906 and is located at the Livermore fire station near San Francisco, California.

Fact 630: The "Diderot effect" is the phenomenon whereby after a purchase some people feel compelled to make further purchases in order to create an appropriate overall picture. If, for example, you buy a new item of clothing, this often leads to dissatisfaction with old items of clothing. You therefore buy clothes that go better with the new garment.

Fact 631: Approximately 4.3 trillion cigarette butts are generated worldwide every year.

Fact 632: The Italian "San Marino" is the oldest republic in the world.

Fact 633: Beards have a health-benefit effect. They prevent pollen from entering the mouth so that the possibility of getting hay fever is decreased.

Fact 634: Airbags deploy completely within approximately 30 milliseconds.

Fact 635: Although apes have already been taught sign language and thus have the ability to answer a human question, no ape has ever asked a question by itself, despite having the necessary vocabulary to do so. Researchers therefore assume that the ability to ask questions requires a high cognitive level. Apes, however, do not seem to have this ability.

Fact 636: An adult oyster can clean and filter up to 190 liters of water per day.

Fact 637: Kiwis are among the smallest birds in the world, but they lay the largest eggs relative to the size of their bodies.

Fact 638: Marvel originally was named "Timely Comics".

Fact 639: Hawaii plans to pass a law by 2024 prohibiting anyone under the age of 100 from smoking cigarettes.

Fact 640: The colder your bedroom is, the higher is the likelihood of having a nightmare.

Fact 641: When James Cameron was in a Roman hospital due to food poisoning he had a nightmare about a robot from the future trying to kill him. From this idea he created the script for "Terminator".

Fact 642: Malaria was once used to treat syphilis. As early as 1917, the Austrian physician Julius Wagner-Jauregg injected syphilis patients with the malaria pathogen in order for the resulting fever to kill the syphilis pathogens. The method of treatment was so successful that Julius Wagner-Jauregg was awarded the Nobel Prize for Medicine in 1927. Since the discovery of penicillin, however, this method of treatment has been abandoned.

Fact 643: In terms of CD sales, Mozart was the most successful musician in 2016.

Fact 644: In an online petition, 87,000 people voted for McDonald's to serve a vegetarian burger.

Fact 645: In 539 BC the Persian king "Cyrus the Great" adopted the first human rights of the world. He thus freed all slaves and gave people the right to decide for themselves what they wanted to do.

Fact 646: The first call with a mobile phone was made by its inventor, Martin Cooper. He called a rival to brag about his achievement.

Fact 647: Once, Charlie Chaplin took part in a Charlie Chaplin imitator contest and came in third place.

Fact 648: The people who voiced Mickey Mouse and Minnie Mouse in the 1930s were married in real life.

Fact 649: The more you burp, the less you have to fart.

Fact 650: When your fingers swell from being underwater too long, it is because of an evolutionary trait of your nervous system. The fingers swell so as to provide more grip in wet conditions.

Fact 651: In 2017, researchers discovered the largest dinosaur footprint to date in Western Australia. The footprint is over 5 feet long and is said to be over 130 million years old.

Fact 652: The longest mathematical proof is more than 15,000 pages long and was written by more than 100 mathematicians.

Fact 653: Shortly before his death, James Barrie, the creator of Peter Pan, transferred the rights to his book to the Great Ormond Street Hospital in London, which today is one of the leading children's hospitals in Britain. To this day, the royalty income from the book continues to support the hospital in treating a large number of children.

Fact 654: Whittier is a city in Alaska with 217 inhabitants. Almost the entire population of the city lives in the small community's only building, which also houses a school, a hospital, a church and a grocery store. For this, the town has been nicknamed the "town under one roof".

Fact 655: Over a billion people still have no access to electricity.

Fact 656: Blowing out the candles on a birthday cake increases the number of bacteria on the cake by around 1,400 percent.

Fact 657: The Sagrada Familia in Barcelona has been under construction for over 130 years and is still not finished.

Fact 658: The oldest high-school graduate in Germany is 73 years old.

Fact 659: The suicide rate in Japan is 60 percent above the global average. This is why workshops teaching people to express their feelings are becoming more and more popular in the country.

Fact 660: When the Egyptians built the pyramids, there were still mammoths roaming the earth.

Fact 661: Robert Williams, a former Ford assembly line worker, was the first human to be killed by a robot. He was fatally hit in the head by a robot arm in 1979.

Fact 662: Regular sex can relieve nasal congestion and help treat asthma and hay fever.

Fact 663: The African continent is the oldest populated area.

Fact 664: The frontman of the punk rock band "The Offspring" ("Pretty Fly for a White Guy") completed his dissertation in molecular biology in 2017.

Fact 665: Anna Bågenholm survived the second lowest body temperature ever recorded in humans. Due to a skiing accident, she was trapped in water under a layer of ice for 80 minutes. Her body temperature dropped to 56.7 degrees Fahrenheit. Although doctors believed her to be clinically dead, she survived the incident without further damage.

Fact 666: After the great success of the Eiffel Tower, London planned the construction of the similar looking Watkin's Tower in 1892. Due to economic difficulties encountered by the construction company, however, the tower was never completed and was later demolished. At over 1.148 feet, it would have been the tallest building of its time.

Fact 667: In Amsterdam there is a gym where you can train naked.

Fact 668: Hugh Hefner has become almost completely deaf in recent years. Doctors believe his increased use of Viagra is the cause. Hefner however, says that he would rather be deaf than forgo sex.

Fact 669: In 2010, Venezuela decided to introduce stricter naming restrictions. Previously, unusual first names were no problem. For example, there are two people with the first name "Superman" living in the South American country - Superman Gonzalez and Superman Fernandez. There are even 60 babies who after their birth were given the first name Hitler.

Fact 670: The word "gym" comes from Greek and translates to "place of the naked."

Fact 671: The "Chewbacca defense" is a term commonly used in the United States for the legal or political defense of a position using nonsensical arguments. The term derives from an episode of the animated series "South Park", in which this defense strategy was used to mock O. J. Simpson's lawyer.

Fact 672: Netflix has over 20 million subscribers in China even though Netflix is not available in China.

Fact 673: In 1913, Adolf Hitler, Joseph Stalin, Leo Trotsky, and Sigmund Freud all lived close to each other in the immediate vicinity of Vienna, and regularly went to the same cafe without ever having come into contact with each other.

Fact 674: The "hyoid bone", a small bone in the oral cavity under the tongue, is the only bone in the human body that is not connected to another bone.

Fact 675: A regular inspection including oil change on a Bugatti Veyron costs 21,000 dollars.

Fact 676: September always begins on the same day of the week as December.

Fact 677: When the moon is furthest away from Earth, both celestial bodies are so far apart that all the planets in our solar system could fit in between.

Fact 678: The "Antarctic Treaty" signed in 1961 stipulates that no country may exploit Antarctica economically or use it militarily. Instead, Antarctica is to be made available to all countries of the world for research purposes.

Fact 679: On June 30th, 2015, there was a leap second. One second was added to the last minute of this day.

Fact 680: "Almost" is the longest word in the English language in which all letters are arranged in alphabetical order.

Fact 681: Australian rower Bobby Pearce won the 1928 Olympic Games against eight other competitors, even though he stopped during the race to let ducks pass in front of him.

Fact 682: Jonas Salk refused to take out a patent on his polio vaccine. He commented that: "There is no patent. Could you patent the sun?"

Fact 683: Most airlines have a policy that the pilot and co-pilot of an aircraft are not allowed to eat the same meal in order to avoid the risk of both pilots suffering from food poisoning.

Fact 684: Instead of using lawn mowers, Google has about 200 goats that graze the grass on the Google site.

Fact 685: Young elephants like to suck on their trunks just like young children like to suck on their thumbs.

Fact 686: YouTube Blocked in Tajikistan After a Video of the President Dancing Goes Viral.

Fact 687: In 2012, the CEO of Lenovo received an annual bonus of three million dollars. Instead of keeping the money for himself, he distributed it among his 10,000 employees.

Fact 688: An American married the Eiffel Tower in 2007.

Fact 689: William Griffith Wilson, the founder of Anonymous Alcoholics, asked for a sip of whiskey on his deathbed.

Fact 690: Scientist support that on Enceladus, a moon of Saturn, streams of water can be found.

Fact 691: The country with the highest population density is Monaco. There, an average of 49,106 people share one square mile.

Fact 692: In a guidebook for spies, the US intelligence agency CIA explained how during the Cold War spies could exchange information using their shoelaces. The message communicated differed depending on how the shoelaces were tied.

Fact 693: On Jupiter and Saturn it rains diamonds.

Fact 694: The highest temperature ever measured in a human body was 115.7 degrees Fahrenheit.

Fact 695: Russia extends over eleven time zones.

Fact 696: Only nine percent of consumers of marijuana are addicted.

Fact 697: Family Guy is prohibited in the following countries: Indonesia, Iran, Vietnam, Taiwan, Egypt, South Africa, South Korea and Malaysia.

Fact 698: The word "mafia" refers to the criminal organization in Sicily. Comparable structures in other regions use their own names like "Camorra" or "Yakuza".

Fact 699: According to a survey from 2008, about 58 percent of British teens believed that Sherlock Homes really existed.

Fact 700: At the beginning of the 20th century, horses created so much dirt with their excrements that cars were regarded as the "green" alternative.

Fact 701: Every year on Valentine's Day, approximately 110 million roses are sold worldwide.

Fact 702: With 2.3 million soldiers, China has the largest army in the world. The USA follows in second place with 1.4 million.

Fact 703: The largest cat in the world had a length of 1.36 yards.

Fact 704: Male narwhals have an ivory horn with a length of up to ten feet on their head.

Fact 705: During a press conference in the 70's a reporter asked Stevie Wonder, what it was like being born blind. He answered "It could have been worse. I could have been born black."

Fact 706: Crickets consist of up to 70 percent protein, while beef steaks contain only 17 to 40 percent protein.

Fact 707: McDonald's is the biggest customer of Coca Cola.

Fact 708: At 386 billion dollars, Austria's gross domestic product in 2016 was lower than the US retail company Walmart's sales revenues for the same year, which was 100 billion dollars higher.

Fact 709: It is a long tradition in Ireland to leave a bottle of beer at the front door for Santa Claus.

Fact 710: Motorway junctions without a precise shape are called "spaghetti junctions".

Fact 711: When Google shut down for five minutes in 2013, the world internet traffic decreased by 40 percent.

Fact 712: Kenneth Bainbridge, scientific director of the Manhattan Project, commented on the first test of a nuclear bomb with "Now we are all sons of bitches".

Fact 713: More than 250,000 millionaires live in New York.

Fact 714: Alexithymia is the inability to perceive one's own feelings and put them into words.

Fact 715: To investigate in a strip club in Seattle, an undercover agent visited the club 160 times and spent 16,835 dollars of tax payer money for at least 130 lap dances. Currently not one single person has been charged in this case.

Fact 716: If you combine the first syllables in the names of the countries "Sweden" and "Denmark" you get the word "Swe-Den". If you combine their second syllables, you get the word "Den-Mark".

Fact 717: Lake Baikal in Russia is home to 20 percent of the world's total unfrozen fresh water.

Fact 718: The human kidney can only produce urine up to a salt content of two percent. Salt water, however, has an average salt content of three percent, so our kidneys have to draw water from the body to lower the salt content of the water they take in. The consequence is that after drinking salt water you die of thirst, even though you have actually consumed water.

Fact 719: Scientists have succeeded in creating a genetic strain of manioc that contains more iron and zinc than conventional plants of this type. The crop is a widespread food source, particularly in Latin America, and with this special breeding it could reduce the problem of zinc and iron deficiency in children within the region.

Fact 720: With about 1 billion people or 15% of the world's population Africa is the second most populous continent.

Fact 721: At Starbucks "laughing" is part of the job description.

Fact 722: According to NASA, Jurassic Park is the seventh best movie in the world, measured in terms of scientific accuracy.

Fact 723: Finland has exactly 187,888 lakes and 179,585 islands. Both are world records in terms of frequency.

Fact 724: After James Cameron saw Star Wars for the first time in 1977, he quit his job as a truck driver and began his career in the film industry.

Fact 725: Water cannot go bad and yet there is always an expiration date on water bottles. The reason for this is that the expiration date does not apply to water, but rather indicates when the plastic bottle starts releasing chemicals into the water.

Fact 726: A study has shown that people with a lot of body hair have on average a higher IQ than people with less body hair.

Fact 727: In 1967 a solar storm almost caused a nuclear war. The charged solar particles caused the US early rocket warning system to fail, so that the Americans first assumed that the Soviet Union had launched a targeted interference attack in order to be able to carry out a nuclear strike on the USA.

Fact 728: The avocado core is also edible and contains even more nutrients than the pulp.

Fact 729: The Titanic II is scheduled to put to sea in 2022, following the route of the original Titanic.

Fact 730: The Prague Town Hall Clock, which went into operation in 1410, is the oldest still functioning astronomical clock in the world. In addition to the time, the clock also shows astronomical correlations, such as the position of the moon in relation to Earth.

Fact 731: Pornhub once started a campaign called "Save the Boobs". For every 30th view in the category "small tit" or "big tit", the company donated one penny to the "Susan G Komen Foundation" - a foundation whose aim it is to cure breast cancer. However, the foundation refused the donation. Therefore, Pornhub tripled the amount of money and donated it to a foundation with a similar purpose.

Fact 732: The black mamba can reach a speed of 12.4 miles per hour.

Fact 733: The first graphics-enabled web browser was developed in 1993.

Fact 734: Tom Hanks brother - Jim Hanks - sounds very much alike his brother, which is why he occasionally does synchronization work for him.

Fact 735: The leaves of the "skeleton flower" become transparent when they come into contact with rain.

Fact 736: In the 1890s Bayer, a pharmaceutical company in Germany, advertised heroine as a medicine.

Fact 737: The FBI kept a 1,400-page file on Albert Einstein because he was suspected of being a Communist.

Fact 738: At a height of 2,717 feet, the Burj Khalifa is the tallest building in the world. Due to the skyscraper's height, the upper floors of the building can swing back and forth by five feet in strong winds.

Fact 739: R2-D2 from Star Wars is called C1-P8 in Italy.

Fact 740: To protest against mechanization during the Industrial Revolution, workers threw their wooden shoes - called sabots - into the machines. This is how the word "sabotage" was born.

Fact 741: Until the 20th century, the Bible explicitly mentioned the existence of unicorns. Psalm 22:22 of the Luther Bible of 1912, for example, reads: "Help me out of the lion's mouth and save me from the unicorns!" Today it is assumed that this is a translation error and should be "wild oxen" instead. Apart from unicorns, however, numerous other mythical creatures such as dragons or a Leviathan continue to be mentioned to this day.

Fact 742: The highest jump of a llama was 3.7 feet, and the record is held by the llama "Caspa".

Fact 743: According to nutritional values, the daily requirement of vitamin B6 can be provided by 2.9 pounds Nutella.

Fact 744: On average, first-borns have the highest IQ among their siblings.

Fact 745: Facebook is blue because the founder Mark Zuckerberg suffers from red-green color blindness.

Fact 746: In Kazan, Russia, there is a "Temple of all Religions". The building contains architectural elements of a variety of religions and was therefore created for people of all faiths.

Fact 747: During the 2002 Soccer World Cup, Ahn Jung-hwan from South Korea scored a goal against Italy in injury time, knocking the Italians out of the World Cup. The next day, his contract with his Italian home club was terminated because the owner said he could not pay the person who had ruined Italian football.

Fact 748: Swans only have one partner in their lifetime.

Fact 749: If you had invested $100 in Bitcoin in 2010, you'd be worth more than $70 million now.

Fact 750: According to current scientific knowledge, it is assumed that about 8,000 years ago all people in Europe were dark skinned, and that a light skin color only developed recently over the course of the past millennia.

Fact 751: With one "bite", blue whales consume up to 1,100 pounds of food or almost half a million calories. Opening the mouth and eating food alone can burn up to 2,000 calories.

Fact 752: The "copy and paste" function was invented in 1973 by programmer Larry Tesler.

Fact 753: On 23 March 1994, Aeroflot flight 593 crashed in a hilly landscape over Siberia, killing 75 people. Recordings on the voice recorder proved that at the time of the accident the pilot had let his 15-year-old son fly the plane.

Fact 754: The continent with the highest average education level is Antarctica.

Fact 755: Genetically, mushrooms are closer to humans than to plants.

Fact 756: After the breeding season, swifts spend up to ten months in the air without landing a single time. With that, they hold the record among birds.

Fact 757: The Japanese company YKK is the largest manufacturer of zippers in the world. That is why the company logo "YKK" can be found on most zippers worldwide.

Fact 758: On its website, Netflix offers the opportunity to request series or films to be included in the company's online catalogue.

Fact 759: On average, children start lying at the age of four.

Fact 760: If men do not ejaculate for more than seven days, their testosterone levels rise by more than 45 percent.

Fact 761: A cross between a zebra and a horse is called a "zorse".

Fact 762: The Liberian presidential election of 1927 is considered to be the most falsified election of all time and even made it into the Guinness Book of World Records. The winner of the election, Charles D. B. King, won with more than 243,000 votes, although there were only 15,000 registered voters.

Fact 763: Crows are among the most intelligent non-primates on earth. They possess the intelligence of a toddler, can use tools, have a long-term memory, can recognize faces and understand analogies.

Fact 764: Male clownfish become females when their partner dies.

Fact 765: Tattooing is illegal in South Korea. In the country, tattoos are mainly worn by criminals, which is why a tattoo is considered a valid reason for a company not to hire somebody.

Fact 766: Marie Curie's scientific notes are still so radioactive that you need to wear a protective suit to look at them safely.

Fact 767: Man has already left over 200 tons of garbage on the moon, including 70 spaceships, backpacks, 96 bags with urine and vomit as well as old boots.

Fact 768: In summer, storks poop on each other's feet in order to cool down.

Fact 769: Under ideal conditions, two mating rats could produce 482 million descendants over a three-year period.

Fact 770: A study came to the conclusion that female students, who are perceived as attractive by their fellow male students, achieve better grades.

Fact 771: According to his driving license, Spongebob was born on July 14, 1986.

Fact 772: From 2015 to 2016, Englishman Ben Smith ran 401 marathons on 401 days to raise money for the victims of bullying. With his "401 Challenge" he set a world record and covered a total of 10,506 miles.

Fact 773: Although the name Tiffany was extremely popular in the 12th century, it is never used in historical novels because readers find it too modern. This has given rise to the term "Tiffany effect", where something is considered much more modern than it actually is.

Fact 774: Big Ben is only the name of the main bell in the belfry of London. The correct name of the bell tower is "Clock Tower".

Fact 775: In order to better investigate the effects of a black widow's poison, the scientist Allan Walker Blair voluntarily let the dangerous spider bite him.

Fact 776: Paparazzi is Italian and can be translated to "annoying mosquitoes".

Fact 777: In order to prevent tickets to his concerts from becoming too expensive, musician Kid Rock charges a maximum of 100,000 dollars per gig.

Fact 778: Gandhi was nominated five times for the Nobel Peace Prize, but never received it.

Fact 779: The chimpanzee "Congo" was able to draw abstract works of art. Even Pablo Picasso was a fan of his pictures.

Fact 780: In 2008, the average age in Uganda was 15. This means that about 50 percent of the population was under the age of 15 at that time.

Fact 781: Theodore Roosevelt is the only US president known to have had a tattoo.

Fact 782: Thursday is named after the Nordic god of thunder "Thor".

Fact 783: Nearly one in five Germans regularly use a laptop on the toilet.

Fact 784: In the past, the sickrooms of cancer patients were always round, as there was a superstition that cancer cells always gathered in the corners of rooms. To this day, you can still find many historic hospitals with round rooms.

Fact 785: The founders of Adidas and Puma were brothers.

Fact 786: In 1976 the BBC made an April fools hoax, that the planets in our sun system are located in a special constellation so that the gravity is decreased. This resulted in more than one thousand calls, confirming that one actually can feel the effect.

Fact 787: In the Middle Ages green was the colour of love.

Fact 788: In order to celebrate her 70th birthday, Kansas City native Chau Smith ran seven marathons on seven continents on seven consecutive days.

Fact 789: Ryan Gosling was short-listed to be in the Backstreet Boys.

Fact 790: While the British royal system allows women who marry into the royal family to become queens, men who marry into the royal family cannot become kings. Men who marry into the family only receive the royal title "Prince". This is the reason why the husband of the reigning Queen Elizabeth is only Prince and not King of the United Kingdom.

Fact 791: In 1987 American Airlines was able to save 40,000 dollars because they used one less olive in their salads.

Fact 792: The official length of a marathon was defined as 26,219 miles because it was exactly the length of the course at the Olympic Games in London in 1908 and not because it corresponds to the historical distance between Athens and Marathon. That distance is only about 24.8 miles.

Fact 793: The fear of long words is called hippopotomonstrosesquipedaliophobia.

Fact 794: In the USA, there is a sports league for rock paper-scissors competitions.

Fact 795: It is genetically determined whether you can role your tongue or not.

Fact 796: A platypus can sense the electric field generated by the muscle movement of its prey. It can therefore sense the prey's movement before it even happens.

Fact 797: The Counter Strike team "Silver Snipers" consists of five members who are between 62 and 81 years old.

Fact 798: A bird of paradise's feathers are so black that they absorb 99.95 percent of all light. This is only 0.01 percentage points less than the blackest material ever created by humans.

Fact 799: It is assumed that cats are responsible for the extinction of several animal species.

Fact 800: Since 1989, the mass of all living insects has decreased by around 76 percent: The causes could be too much fertilizer in agriculture, a reduction in the amount of available green space and climate change.

Fact 801: Pingelap is a Western Pacific island atoll where two thirds of the inhabitants are color-blind.

Fact 802: Megatherium was a giant sloth that was 20 feet long, had huge claws to defend itself and weighed as much as an elephant. Thanks to small bone plates under its skin, it was armored as if by chain mail.

Fact 803: In third world countries, residents can access Wikipedia via their smartphone without using their data. The "Wikipedia Zero" campaign is already available in 34 countries.

Fact 804: In 2016, there was a new billionaire in China every five days.

Fact 805: Most serial killers are born in November.

Fact 806: All faces we see in our dreams are faces of people we have already met in real life.

Fact 807: When leaving school, a child in the U.S. has already witnessed 40,000 people dying on TV.

Fact 808: Israel is the only country in the world that has seen a net increase in trees over the last 100 years.

Fact 809: If you Google "elgooG", you will get to a mirrored Google.

Fact 810: The Batman series from the 1960s was known for its educational themes. The viewers were invited to fasten their seatbelts in the car, do homework, drink milk and eat healthily.

Fact 811: About 89 percent of all men have problems with differentiating between kind behavior from a woman and flirting.

Fact 812: The Small World Phenomenon states that every person on the planet is connected to every other person through a short chain of only six acquaintances

Fact 813: Miguel Indurain, five times Tour de France winner, has a resting heart rate of 28 beats per minute.

Fact 814: To avoid baggage fees, a man from China wore 70 items of clothing on his body.

Fact 815: Russian man, Valery Spiridonov was alleged to be the first human to receive a head transplant. His head was to be transplanted to a new body, but he decided against it after a long hesitation. Meanwhile, a Chinese man that hasn't been named is to take his place.

Fact 816: The Wall of China cannot be seen from space - however, China's smog can.

Fact 817: Human fingers are so sensitive that they can feel objects of 13 nanometers in size. This means that if one finger was the size of the earth, it could feel the difference between a house and a car.

Fact 818: The "Book of Mormon", the religious foundation of the Mormon faith, which is close to Christianity, tells of a colonization of America in the time of Christ. The country is described as having always been rich in food and animals. Among other things, cattle, sheep, horses, pigs, goats, elephants, wheat and barley are mentioned. According to the latest scientific findings, however, these things only came to America with the colonization by Columbus.

Fact 819: The name of the US state of Louisiana dates back to the time of the French colony of New France in the 18th century. It stretched from the Gulf of Mexico far into northern Canada to Newfoundland. The part south of the Great Lakes was called Louisiana in honor of Louis XIV - Louis Quatorze in French. Today's state on the Gulf of Mexico has only a fraction of this size, but continues to bear this name.

Fact 820: Since 1964, in memory of the victims of the atomic bomb, the "flame of peace" is burning in Hiroshima, which will only be extinguished once all nuclear weapons on the earth have been eliminated.

Fact 821: Porn actress Lisa Sparxxx holds the world record for the highest number of sex partners within 24 hours. In 2004, during her attempt to set a new record, she had sex with 919 different men in one day.

Fact 822: English is the only globally recognized language in airspace. All pilots must speak this language, regardless of their country of origin.

Fact 823: By his own account, the former Yugoslav King Alexander I avoided public appearances on Tuesdays because too many family members had already been murdered on this day of the week. However, when it could no longer be avoided and he had to appear publicly in Marseille on Tuesday, 9 October 1934, he was shot by the Bulgarian Vladimir Chernozemski.

Fact 824: "Trimethylaminuria" is a metabolic disease that causes the patient to smell strongly of old fish.

Fact 825: In South Africa there is a bar in a 6,000 year old tree.

Fact 826: The bikini was named after the bikini atoll, a group of islands on which the United States carried out its atomic bomb tests. The inventor Louis Réard chose the name because he thought the bikini was small and stunning.

Fact 827: In terms of the number of museums, theatres and libraries, Germany is the country with the most opportunities for cultural activities.

Fact 828: Microsoft sued the student Mike Rowe after he launched the site MikeRowSoft.com.

Fact 829: The term "cross sea" is used to describe a phenomenon in which waves from different directions meet and produce a rectangular wave pattern.

Fact 830: Santa Claus was not invented by Coca Cola.

Fact 831: The first person shooter "Half Life" has already been successfully used in the treatment of arachnophobia (the fear of spiders).

Fact 832: In Switzerland there are dishwashers with cheese fondue and raclette programs.

Fact 833: The word "alphabet" consists of the words "alpha" and "beta", which are the first two letters in the Greek alphabet.

Fact 834: Tibetan monks sleep while sitting.

Fact 835: Researchers in Australia are working on a new condom made of cellulose that is 30 percent thinner but 20 percent more robust.

Fact 836: When California was exposed to an extreme drought in 1915, a "rainmaker" was hired by the City of San Diego and promised a payment of 10,000 dollars if he managed to summon rain. Shortly thereafter it rained for almost a month without interruption, resulting in numerous floods and destroyed dams. The city council decided that this must have been a sign from God, so they did not pay the rainmaker.

Fact 837: The Christmas tree was invented in Germany.

Fact 838: Will Smith was originally supposed to play the role of Neo in "Matrix". However, he refused and preferred to do "Wild Wild West" instead.

Fact 839: With the Active Denial System, the United States already has a microwave weapon that can heat the skin of victims up to 0.3 miles away to 55 degrees in just a few seconds.

Fact 840: Nintendo means "temple of heavenly responsibility".

Fact 841: Every year around 600 lightning bolts strike the Statue of Liberty.

Fact 842: September was originally the seventh month of the year. The name comes from the Latin word "septem", which means "seven".

Fact 843: The largest ant colony in the world was discovered in 2002 and contains several billion animals. The superstate has many millions of nests and stretches over 3,580 miles from the Italian Riviera to the northwest of Spain.

Fact 844: The intelligence of a child is primarily determined by its mother.

Fact 845: The inventor of "Spongebob" Stephen Hillenburg was a marine biologist, which is why he chose the deep sea as the setting for his cartoon series.

Fact 846: Rome holds the world record for the city with most elevators.

Fact 847: In New Zealand, there is a lake, which on average has a temperature of 147 degrees Fahrenheit due to geothermal processes.

Fact 848: The fur of a mammoth could grow to a length of more than three feet in winter.

Fact 849: Renfield-Syndrome is characterized by an obsession with drinking blood.

Fact 850: The full name of Mr. Burns is Charles Montgomery Plantagenet Schicklgruber Burns.

Fact 851: To celebrate its 50th birthday, around 300,000 people crossed the Golden Gate Bridge simultaneously on 24 May 1987. This resulted in the bridge sinking by 3.2 feet.

Fact 852: The video game "Super Mario Bros." was so popular in 1985 that the best-selling book in Japan was a guidebook containing tips on how best to play the game.

Fact 853: About 60 million people who are alive today, will die within the next 12 months.

Fact 854: Almost 40% of all adults on Africa are illiterate.

Fact 855: From water depth of 33 feet and more there is no more red light. For this reason blood seems to be green at this depth.

Fact 856: The fake cocaine that actors snort in movies is usually white snuff. It does not contain any real tobacco, but usually only consists of a mix of dextrose and menthol.

Fact 857: The movie "French Kiss" is called "English Kiss" in France.

Fact 858: There is a woman whose name is actually "Marijuana Pepsi Jackson". The African-American woman now carries the surname Vandyck and wrote her dissertation on unusual black names in the classroom.

Fact 859: Hippopotamus kill more Africans than lions, crocodiles and white sharks combined.

Fact 860: The Japanese giant crab is the largest living crab and can reach a span of up to 12.1 feet. However, the body has an average diameter of only 14.6 inches.

Fact 861: New York is located more southern than Rome.

Fact 862: Bob Marley's wife Rita was shot in the head in an assassination attempt in 1976. Due to the thickness of her dreadlocks, however, she survived the incident.

Fact 863: Spain and Morocco are only separated by 9 miles (15km).

Fact 864: When two wolves mate, they stay together for the rest of their lives.

Fact 865: According to a study, men from Congo have the largest penises.

Fact 866: Blind people are able to dream and to see pictures in their dreams.

Fact 867: In 1994, Microsoft, in collaboration with Timex, introduced the world's first smart watch. At that time, however, nobody was interested in it, so production was discontinued.

Fact 868: It is impossible to sneeze with your eyes open.

Fact 869: In 1952 Albert Einstein received the offer to become President of Israel. He refused.

Fact 870: The weirdest things that have been found in food sold by McDonald's are: bandaging material, the head of a chicken and a dead rat.

Fact 871: During the Olympic Games in China, Usain Bolt ate only chicken nuggets, as it was the only meal he recognized from home. Ultimately, he won three gold medals with this diet.

Fact 872: If you have a ten dollar note in your pocket and do not have any debts, you are richer than 25 percent of the U.S. citizens.

Fact 873: If you cook a penguin egg, the egg white remains transparent after cooking.

Fact 874: Papua New Guinea is the country with the greatest variety of languages spoken in a single country. Although the country has only about eight million inhabitants, more than 700 different languages are spoken.

Fact 875: Dick Hoyt and his son Rick, who is fully paralyzed, have participated in countless sporting events under the name "Team Hoyt". The two even completed six Iron Man events together. Dick first swam 2.5 miles, pulling his son in a boat behind him, then rode a bicycle over the roads for 112 miles, before pushing him in a wheelchair for another 26.2 miles.

Fact 876: During World War I the Emperor of Germany, the King of Great Britain and the Emperor of Russia were all first cousins. The German Emperor Wilhelm II therefore commented sarcastically on the First World War: "If our grandmother (Queen Victoria) were still alive, she would never have allowed it."

Fact 877: Google's first tweet was "I'm 01100110 01100101 01100101 01101100 01101001 01101110 01100111 00100000 01101100 01110101 01100011 01101011 01111001 00001010" which is binary code for "I'm feeling lucky".

Fact 878: The full name of Yoshi is T. Yoshisaur Munchakoopas.

Fact 879: Every year on 13 October, Finland celebrates the official day of failure.

Fact 880: One bite of the Inland-Taipans - the most poisonous snake in the world - injects enough poison into its victim to kill more than 230 people.

Fact 881: Jakarta is the fastest sinking city in the world. Every year, the ground sinks by up to ten inches.

Fact 882: If you close your eyes and try to walk straight, you are involuntarily inclined to walk in circles. There is currently no explanation found by scientists as to why this happens.

Fact 883: On the small island of Limone sul Garda in Italy the inhabitants have developed a genetic mutation that makes it impossible for them to have a heart attack.

Fact 884: Adolescents are increasingly suffering from sleep deprivation. The reason for this is, among other things, the early start of school.

Fact 885: Jack Daniel's now also sells whiskey-flavored coffee beans.

Fact 886: Since Penélope Cruz was pregnant during the shooting of "Pirates of the Caribbean: On Stranger Tides", her sister Mónica Cruz, who is three years younger, stepped in as her body double.

Fact 887: Vikings took cats on sea trips in order to avoid a rat problem. Nowadays, it is assumed that this prevailed the worldwide spread of cats.

Fact 888: A Pinocchio paradox arises when Pinocchio says "My nose is currently growing" and is an example of the more general liar paradox. This refers to a sentence that describes its own statement as false, such as "This sentence is false."

Fact 889: So far, there have already been around 106 billion people in the world.

Fact 890: Ötzi suffered from lactose intolerance.

Fact 891: Mars is the only known planet which is inhabited solely by robots.

Fact 892: NASA has two identical satellites orbiting the Earth and repeatedly measuring the distance between each other to detect gravitational deviations. They are nicknamed "Tom" and "Jerry" because one satellite is always "chasing" the other.

Fact 893: Kopi luwak is the most expensive coffee in the world. It is produced by feeding the beans to civets, which break down the bitter substances in the beans during their digestive process. The otherwise intact beans are collected after excretion and prepared for sale.

Fact 894: It has been known since 1971 that the Olympus Mons volcano on Mars is the largest known volcano in our solar system. By comparison, it was not until 2013 that the largest volcano on Earth was discovered: the Tamu Massif in the Pacific.

Fact 895: Karaoke is Japanese and means "empty orchestra".

Fact 896: The Jewish population is only 0.2 percent, yet 20 percent of all Nobel prizes have been awarded to people of the Jewish faith.

Fact 897: The drug lord Pablo Escobar had so much cash in his home that rats ate about a billion dollars of his wealth per year.

Fact 898: The unit of one "meter" was first introduced during the French Revolution and was defined as one ten-millionth of the distance between the North Pole and the equator.

Fact 899: The credit for the loudest burp ever goes to Englishman Paul Hunn, whose burp on 23 August 2009 was measured at 109.9 decibels, which corresponds to the volume at a rock concert.

Fact 900: When we talk to somebody we like, our voice changes.

Fact 901: A 20 second hug increases the oxytocin level of people so much that afterwards there is a much greater trust between them.

Fact 902: With a height of 380.3 feet, the highest tree in the world is the sequoia "Hyperion" in the Redwood National Park in California.

Fact 903: The true inventor of the first practical light bulb was not Thomas Alva Edison, but Joseph Wilson Swan. He had already secured a patent for his invention in England two years before Edison. But the two eventually reached an out-of-court agreement and joined forces in the Edison & Swan United Electric Light Company.

Fact 904: The Norwegian Hans Lengseth holds the record for the world's longest beard. His beard had a total length of 17.5 feet.

Fact 905: One of the founders of the DNA structure - James Watson - was forced to sell his Nobel Prize in 2014 due to financial problems. He received 4.1 million dollars and the buyer gave him the Nobel Prize back afterwards.

Fact 906: In 1938, Adolf Hitler was Time Magazine's "Person of the Year".

Fact 907: In 1994 a man was arrested in Los Angeles for scaring elderly people. He dressed himself as the grim reaper and looked inside the windows of the elderly.

Fact 908: Between 2011 and 2013, China consumed more cement than the USA during the entire 20th century.

Fact 909: Parkinson's Law describes the fact that an employee needs as much time for a task as he has available for it.

Fact 910: In 2011, a high school in Chicago launched a special type of fundraising campaign. In the breaks between lessons, the Justin Bieber song "Baby" was played over and over again in the school and the students had to donate money to have the song stopped.

Fact 911: Physicist Nikola Tesla is said to have had an eidetic (photographic) memory and spoke eight different languages fluently: Serbo-Croatian, Czech, English, French, German, Hungarian, Italian and Latin. Even Albert Einstein was convinced that Tesla was more intelligent than he was.

Fact 912: Water only gets the typical chlorine smell when someone pees in the basin.

Fact 913: The real name of actor Michael Keaton is Michael Douglas.

Fact 914: To date, there have been a total of 2,055 atomic bomb tests worldwide. 1,039 were carried out by the USA alone, 718 by the Soviet Union and 198 by France.

Fact 915: In almost all of his songs, Lenny Kravitz does not only sing, but also plays all instruments in a recording studio.

Fact 916: The gravity on the moon is about one-sixth of the earth's gravitational pull.

Fact 917: NASA claims it will be able to answer the question if we are alone in universe in the next 20 years.

Fact 918: The name "England" derives from the old English term "Englaland", which means "Land of the Angles".

Fact 919: The designer Ko Yang has invented a milk package that changes its color when the milk begins to spoil.

Fact 920: In 1930 Ketchup was sold as medicine.

Fact 921: Sound spreads through steel about 15 times faster than through air.

Fact 922: In 2014 a woman was saved from her burning house. She then realized she had forgot her mobile phone in the house, ran back into her home and died.

Fact 923: There is actually a website about Barney Stinson's fake character "Lorenzo von Matterhorn" from "How I Met Your Mother": www.lorenzovonmatterhorn.com.

Fact 924: Josef Stalin ordered at least 22 assassination attempts on the former Yugoslav President Josip Broz Tito. After his death, a letter to Stalin with the following words was discovered: "Stop sending people to kill me. If you don't stop sending assassins, I will send one to Moscow and I will certainly not have to send a second one."

Fact 925: Werner Forßmann performed the world's first cardiac catheterization. Since he was not allowed to carry out such a risky experiment on patients, he tested the method on himself. With the tube reaching through his arm into his heart, he then went to the hospital's X-ray department and proved with the resulting evidence that heart catheters are possible on humans. Due to the high risk he had taken with this procedure, he was fired from the hospital. 27 years later, he was awarded the Nobel Prize for Medicine.

Fact 926: It would require 1,200,000 mosquitoes to exsanguinate the blood out of a human.

Fact 927: US President John F. Kennedy was a passionate smoker. In 1962, he instructed his press officer to buy 1,000 Cuban cigars for him. Shortly after receiving the cigars, he went on to pass a law prohibiting the import of communist goods into the United States.

Fact 928: In England, the second Day of Christmas is called "Boxing Day" because employees and servants traditionally received a gift box - the so-called Christmas Box - from their employer.

Fact 929: In Amazon's early days, there was a programming error that caused Amazon to pay money to its customers. All you had to do was buy a negative number of books, and the amount was credited to your credit card.

Fact 930: Liliy's high school lover, Scooter from "How I Met Your Mother" , is the husband of Barney actor - Neil Patrick Harris - in real life.

Fact 931: In Cambodia you can buy pizzas with marijuana as a topping. It is called Happy Pizza.

Fact 932: With total assets of 1.5 billion dollars, Snapchat founder Evan Spiegel is the world's youngest billionaire.

Fact 933: In the Turkish village Halfeti, completely black roses grow each summer.

Fact 934: The term "money laundering" can be traced back to Al Capone, as he used Laundromats for this purpose.

Fact 935: Kirani James was the first Olympian to win a gold medal for his home country Grenada. His homeland was so proud of it that there was a huge celebration for him and he was rewarded with over 220,000 euros. Today he can even be found on the country's stamps, a stadium bears his name and his hometown opened a museum about his achievements.

Fact 936: In order to make wolf puppies urinate, their mother has to lick their bellies with her warm tongue.

Fact 937: According to a report by the World Bank and the United Nations, around 5.6 million children under the age of five died in 2016. Most of them did not even survive the first weeks after birth. The devastating medical conditions that continue to prevail in many parts of the world result in a rapid spread of infectious diseases without the possibility of treatment. Hunger also plays an important role in these statistics.

Fact 938: The name "Microsoft" is a combination of "microcomputer" and "software".

Fact 939: In 1940, two Australian planes crashed into each other during an Air Force training flight. The planes were wedged into each other so tightly that the pilot of the upper plane was able to land both planes safely. None of the passengers were injured.

Fact 940: "Son of Sam Law" is the term used in the USA to describe laws that prohibit criminals from earning money in any way with the stories of their crimes - for example through films or books. Instead, the state has the right to confiscate such proceeds and pay the money to the perpetrator's victims.

Fact 941: Algeria is not just the largest country in Africa but also among the then largest countries in the world.

Fact 942: When Ed Headrick, the inventor of the Frisbee, died in 2002, his ashes were melted down into Frisbees and distributed to his family and closest friends.

Fact 943: In September 1719, prisoners in Paris were released under the condition that they marry a prostitute and emigrate to Louisiana, USA. The objective was to advance French colonies along the Mississippi.

Fact 944: Marie Byrd Land in Antarctica and Bir Tawil, an area between Egypt and Sudan, are the only areas in the world that do not belong to a nation. These areas are therefore no man's land.

Fact 945: The combination of a knife with a fork and a spoon is called spork.

Fact 946: The Cristo Redentor statue in Rio de Janeiro is not the largest Christ statue in the world. With a height of 108 feet, the Christ the King statue in Poland is ten feet higher.

Fact 947: Barney Stinson from "How I met your Mother" is the real inventor of the "Bro-Code". Based on Google search analytics the term hadn't existed before 2008.

Fact 948: During the so called "scramble for Africa" all of Africa was colonized by foreign powers, except for Liberia and Ethiopia.

Fact 949: The original name of "Bank of America" was "Bank of Italy".

Fact 950: Scientists have demonstrated that cats have the same brain patterns as humans have during sleep. It is therefore assumed that cats can dream.

Fact 951: The Towers of the World Trade Centre had their own zip code: 10048 New York.

Fact 952: In 2018, a message in a bottle was found in Australia which had been dropped into the Indian Ocean by a German research vessel in 1886.

Fact 953: The Belgian Post Office developed a special stamp in 2013 that tastes like chocolate when licked on the back.

Fact 954: Koala bears, monkeys and humans are the only animals with an individual fingerprint.

Fact 955: In 1972 the first black superhero to get his own comic book series, Luke Cage was released.

Fact 956: The Bourbon vanilla takes its name from the island of Réunion, where the black pods are grown. After the occupation by the French King Louis XIII, the island was called "Bourbon" after the name of his noble family.

Fact 957: Starbucks was named after the first mate of Captain Ahab in Moby Dick.

Fact 958: During the Second World War, the US Army maintained a tactical deception unit. It consisted of numerous artists, film set designers and actors. Their task was to create vehicle dummies and to simulate operations. Soldiers called their friends in this unit the "Ghost Army".

Fact 959: The center line of the football stadium in Macapá, Brazil, is exactly on the equator line, so that the competing teams in a match are always on different hemispheres.

Fact 960: As early as 1966 Ford released the first electric car, which had a range of more than 200 miles. A sodium-sulphur accumulator was used as a battery. After an accident in rainy weather, the hot sodium leaking from the battery mixed with water and ignited. There was a fire that was difficult to extinguish. As a result, the model was reset and sodium-sulphur batteries were no longer used in vehicles.

Fact 961: A U.S. court had to decide if the X-men are humans or not. In the US, imported dolls representing human beings are subject to a higher tax than other toys. As of this a toy manufacturer sued for a declaration that the action figures did not represent human beings to pay lower taxes.

Fact 962: When the head of the Auschwitz concentration camp - Rudolf Höß - was accused in court of killing 3.5 million people, he replied "No, only two and a half million. The rest died of disease and hunger."

Fact 963: The sign "Made in Germany" was originally intended to warn British people of inferior items from Germany.

Fact 964: Japanese shops have small balls filled with orange die in their tills. In the event of a theft, the store staff can throw the balls at the robber, who is then marked with the orange color for the police.

Fact 965: In 2007, Navy SEAL Mike Day was shot 27 times by four al-Qaeda leaders. He managed to kill the four leaders and get himself to safety. Today, he is in good health again and lives happily with his wife and daughter.

Fact 966: In 1916, a law was submitted to the US Congress to stipulate that any declaration of war by the USA first had to be confirmed by a referendum and that anyone who voted "yes" would have to go to war themselves. However, the law was never passed.

Fact 967: The "Drinkable Book" contains instructions on how to filter your water properly. At the same time, it consists of separable pages with integrated silver particles that can eliminate around 99 percent of the bacteria in contaminated water. Each book has so many pages that it can supply a person with clean water for up to four years.

Fact 968: Oxford University is older than the civilization of the Aztecs.

Fact 969: 450 men die of breast cancer in the U.S. each year.

Fact 970: In Uganda there is a kingdom called Buganda and its national language is Luganda.

Fact 971: In Japan, a restaurant called "The Restaurant Of Order Mistakes" was opened. The restaurant's waiters all suffer from dementia, so visitors never know if they will really get what they ordered.

Fact 972: In Iran 70 percent of all science students are female.

Fact 973: At least 50 percent of the oxygen in our atmosphere is produced by phytoplankton in the oceans and not by land plants. Due to the rising sea temperatures, however, the phytoplankton population continues to decline.

Fact 974: The blue whale is the loudest animal on earth. Its cries can be heard from a distance of 373 miles.

Fact 975: There is a garbage island floating in the Pacific that is three times the size of France and consists of about 88,000 tons of plastic.

Fact 976: Around 75 percent of all vehicles, which were produced by Rolls-Royce, are still in operation.

Fact 977: According to current knowledge, the Earth is the only known planet on which a fire can burn. None of the other known planets have enough oxygen for this.

Fact 978: Che Guevara's first name was actually Ernesto. In Argentina and other Latin American countries, the interjection "Che" is used to get the attention of the person you are talking to, similar to "right?" or "isn't it?" in English. As Ernesto used this linguistic peculiarity frequently, he was soon only referred to as "El Che" following his formative trip to Guatemala.

Fact 979: It is estimated that every five seconds, somebody somewhere in the world buys a BILLY shelf.

Fact 980: 2,520 is the smallest number that can be divided by all numbers from 1 to 10 with the result being an integer, meaning that there is no remainder.

Fact 981: In order to avoid an association with the political Black Panther party, Marvel renamed superhero "Black Panther" to "Black Leopard" for a while.

Fact 982: Many different bacteria are located in a woman's vagina. Much of those bacteria are also found in yogurt.

Fact 983: In 2008, North Korea spent about a quarter of its gross domestic product on the military.

Fact 984: It is unknown where Mozart was buried exactly.

Fact 985: Studies conducted by the University of Michigan have shown a clear correlation between physical exercise and personal satisfaction. According to these studies, one training session per week is sufficient to sustainably increase the feeling of happiness. In addition, exercise is the most efficient way to reduce stress hormones.

Fact 986: To kill a spider, a woman in Kansas burned down her house.

Fact 987: Popcorn became a popular cinema snack in the United States during the global economic crisis because it was so cheap.

Fact 988: In 2017, a Swedish express train was given the name "Trainy McTrainface".

Fact 989: The minute takes its name from the Latin phrase "pars minuta", which means "diminished part" and aims to describe the minute as being the smaller unit of time of the hour. The second was then called "pars minuta secunda", which means "second diminished part" and thus describes the next smaller unit of time.

Fact 990: An average vagina is three to four inches deep and can increase by up to 200 percent when the woman is aroused.

Fact 991: Approximately 20 percent of the French landmass is outside of Europe. For example the islands Martinique and Guadeloupe are in the Caribbean Sea.

Fact 992: Between 2011 and 2013, McDonald's has opened one branch a day in China.

Fact 993: The first digital camera was invented back in 1975 by a Kodak employee. However, the company dropped the idea as it was assumed that it would negatively impact the sale of film rolls.

Fact 994: Depending on the cause of crying, tears have a different chemical composition.

Fact 995: A red hair color paired with blue eyes is the rarest combination of hair and eye color. Only one percent of the world's population has these characteristics.

Fact 996: If you feel very connected to a person, you can hear their voice in your head when you read messages they have sent.

Fact 997: Eminem holds the world record for the most words in a song. At a length of six minutes and four seconds, the song "Rap God" has a total of 1,560 words, resulting in an average of 4.28 words per second.

Fact 998: The DNA among humans differs by just 0.1 percent. In comparison, a chimpanzee is genetically different from humans by 1.2 percent.

Fact 999: In India, forest workers wear masks with a picture of a human face on their back of the heads so that they are not attacked by tigers.

Fact 1000: The maximum speed of a T.Rex was slower than the average sprinting speed of a human.